BOSTON
FIRE DEPARTMENT

RICHARD CONNELLY

outskirtspress
DENVER, COLORADO

This book is dedicated to my only son, Rick, Jr.
who is approaching ten years on the Hingham, MA Fire Department
as a Firefighter/Paramedic.

Pay attention! Stay safe!
Always remain 'OCD' about everything you do!
(It's not a bad thing!)

– Dad

Contents

Foreword i

Section One: The Boston Fire Department 1
Chapter 1   Fire! 3
Chapter 2   Ten Firefighting Myths 13
Chapter 3   Fire Buffs, Sparks, Fire Fans 55
Chapter 4   Arson in Boston 61
Chapter 5   The Boston Fire Department Work Schedule 73
Chapter 6   My Appointment 78

Section Two: Engine 29 85
Chapter 7   Assigned to Engine 29 87
Chapter 8   District 11 90
Chapter 9   The Chief Was Jumping Up and Down in the Street 93
Chapter 10 All of the Chiefs in District 11 Were Characters 98
Chapter 11 Brighton Characters 105
Chapter 12 I've Done My Time 108

Section Three: Ladder 20 113
Chapter 13 Engine 43 and Ladder 20 115
Chapter 14 The Firefighting Finn Family 120
Chapter 15 Lieutenant Jim Dailey 122

Chapter 16   Drive or Tiller? 125
Chapter 17   The Hotel Vendome Tragedy 129
Chapter 18   My Special Vacation 134
Chapter 19   Tales from the Columbia Point Project 136
Chapter 20   I Burned Da Okra! 154
Chapter 21   The Clements Family and Captain Bob Regan 157
Chapter 22   Captain David F. Watkins, Engine Company 39 159
Chapter 23   Cheeseburger, Cheeseburger 165
Chapter 24   You Need a Program to Tell the Characters 167
Chapter 25   Here's Looking at Ya, Kid 171
Chapter 26   Building Fire on Vinton Street 174
Chapter 27   Three-deckers 176
Chapter 28   Ward Court 179
Chapter 29   Jumper on the 22nd Floor 183
Chapter 30   Snow and Winter 186
Chapter 31   The Blizzard of '78 188
Chapter 32   The Drunken Tailgater 195
Chapter 33   I've Got Seven Kids! 197
Chapter 34   Wet Hose, Dry Hose 200
Chapter 35   Boston's White Elephant Ladder Truck 204
Chapter 36   Lieutenant James D. 'Jimbo' Kennedy 208
Chapter 37   The Hurst Tool 212
Chapter 38   Firefighter John T. Aleks 214
Chapter 39   Boston: Automobile Arson Capitol 217
Chapter 40   Deputy Fire Chief George Thompson 219
Chapter 41   Marine Unit Not Needed 228
Chapter 42   But Santa Does It Every Year 230
Chapter 43   Lieutenant Paul Lentini and FF Jimmy Gibbons 232
Chapter 44   Layoffs, Company Closings and Kevin White 235

Section Four: Ladder 7 241
Chapter 45   Welcome to Ladder 7 243
Chapter 46   Meeting House Hill 247
Chapter 47   Firefighter Jack Brignoli 252

Chapter 48   Firefighter Edward R. 'Eddie' Connolly 256
Chapter 49   District Fire Chief Vincent A. Bolger............................ 260
Chapter 50   Batman and Robin 269
Chapter 51   St. Ambrose Church 272
Chapter 52   Tragic Senseless Deaths in the Line of Duty............... 275
Chapter 53   My Return to Division One.. 278
Chapter 54   The Liars Club 280

About the Author 283

Foreword

In this book I have attempted to enlighten the civilians with a view of the fire service. The Boston Fire Department in particular. I have also tried to entertain the members of the fire service whose only experiences may be their very own.

I have attempted humor, but rest assured that many of the tales are serious and heartbreaking memories of fires and of characters who entered my life throughout my career.

The characters that I describe are real and in most cases their real names are used. Only in a few instances where someone may be embarrassed do I attempt to camouflage their real identities.

With the exception of the first few chapters most of the chapters are short with anecdotal type stories from the past and from my memory (while it lasts).

My career spanned six decades and took me to fires over 42 years. This book covers my first 17 years, the years before promotion when I was a grunt, a firefighter on the 'back step'.

I truly believe that there is something in here for every one of you, whether you are a firefighter, company officer, chief officer, civilian or politician.

I want to thank Bill Noonan, Boston Fire Department Photographer, Retired for the photos contained in this book and for the cover photo, as well.

Please write and let me know how you feel. You can contact me at www.outskirtspress.com/characterstalesandtragedies or email me at rick.connelly@verizon.net

Stay safe and be proud!

Richard 'Rick' Connelly
Stow, MA 2014

Section One
The Boston Fire Department

CHAPTER 1

Fire!

"There is something going on down the street!"

Are you the type to go about your business or do you become nosy?

"I think there is a fire. I hear people hollering and now I hear sirens."

Have you ever had the opportunity to be at a fire scene?

"I think it might be a fire!"

When did you arrive?

"Hurry, let's go down there!"

Were you there before the first fire apparatus arrived?

"Here come the fire engines."

Did you come upon the scene during the height of the blaze?

"Oh look. That house is on fire!"

Maybe you arrived after the fire was knocked down.

"Oh, goodness! There was a fire there!"

Depending upon when you arrive you may witness different operations. Early on in the fire you may see a firefighter on the roof cutting a hole in the roof. You may notice the firefighter lean over the side of a flat-roofed building and break the windows on the top floor. A firefighter on a ground ladder may be venting the windows on the upper floors.

These firefighters are all trying to accomplish one thing: ventilation. Venting a fire means giving the smoke, heat and toxic gases a route to exit the building. If victims are reportedly still in the building, this ventilation effort may give them some additional seconds for a searching firefighting team to reach them.

The interior fire attack team advancing a hose line down a hallway into a bedroom needs ventilation. The ventilation act gives the heat, smoke and fire products somewhere to go as they are being pushed by the attack team's hose line.

You see the hose in the street, ladders thrown to the building, water being applied to the fire, lines being advanced into the building, windows being broken, holes being cut in the roof.

You have probably never witnessed the advancement of a hose line into a fire building. It is a marvel to see a couple of firefighters pulling, struggling and dragging a line of hose up a couple of flights of stairs; check the door to the fire apartment for heat; and then crawl down a hallway or through a bedroom. This dragging, checking and crawling is all performed while the apartment is heavily charged with heat and smoke banked down to within a foot or so of the floor.

Conditions are worsening by the second. These conditions exhaust the firefighters. They begin consuming their air at quantities which cannot last too long. They will have to bail out for a bottle change. Going out for more air gives the fire the second breath it is looking for.

What is it that this attack team sees? Quite honestly, *nothing*! The room is hot, dark and mysteriously quiet. Rather than operate the nozzle into smoke, the nozzle man may stop and listen for a second or two. What is it that he is listening for? Primarily he is listening for a sound, a human sound, such as a cry for help or a moaning sound of a fire victim in an extremely perilous predicament.

Many fire victims have been discovered by firefighters performing a search and rescue operation in this manner. Other times a person may be discovered after the smoke has rendered him or her unconscious. Occasionally a victim is discovered quite by accident as the attack team is advancing their line into the fire area.

At least one firefighter from a ladder company may be on the search team. As the firefighter crawls through the apartment he is listening and feeling. Another thing he listens for is the sound of the fire. Fire crackles and makes its own sounds of life.

If you have seen the movie *Backdraft*, you may remember the character played by Robert Deniro (Arson investigator Donald Rimgale) as he explained to the rookie firefighter (Brian McCaffrey played by Billy Baldwin).

"Fire is alive. It eats, it breathes. You have to think like it."

Fire is alive. It does eat, it does breathe. It eats the flammable materials that it encounters. It breathes the oxygen that it feeds on and it chooses its path of travel by finding the easiest, most plausible way to advance.

When fire comes to a barricade on its route of travel, it finds another route. Its usual route is in a vertical path, however when it reaches an obstacle to vertical travel it will travel horizontally until it can resume its vertical travel.

When the fire cannot travel in a vertical path any longer it spreads out horizontally. It continues in that horizontal direction until it no longer has any place to go and then it starts to bank down. This is called mushrooming.

If you think about the scenario I just described, up, out and down, you perhaps can picture a mushroom. This is dangerous, this is when the fire starts to burn back down engulfing the entire room or structure.

These facts are the reasoning behind firefighters opening the roof, opening up walls and performing what is perceived to be 'damage' to a building. The civilian does not understand the importance of opening the vertical route for the fire to burn up and out. Ventilation prevents the spread of fire and enables the interior attack team to enter and get water on the fire therefore aiding in the extinguishment of the free burning fire.

♪♪♪♪

If you have ever made the call for help, you probably thought that it was an eternity before you started hearing the sirens, which signaled the arrival of the fire companies. In reality it was probably no longer than three to five minutes.

It is the aim of every major city's fire department to arrive at the scene of an emergency within four minutes of the call. Some rural areas may see a longer response time due a number of factors. These factors range from a longer travel distance to the minimal staffing due to a volunteer or paid-on-call type of fire department.

Basically there are three types of fire service organizations: Some towns, like major cities, have a paid, on-duty staff which responds to emergencies immediately upon receipt of the notification. Large cities may have a number of fire stations distributed throughout the city. Smaller towns may have only one firehouse.

Quite common today is the arrangement you may find in suburban departments. These towns probably had a paid-on-call type of fire department where the firefighters responded from their homes when the whistle blew. Over the years the whistles have stopped blowing, because the personnel are in contact with the dispatcher with pagers that are activated when a call comes in.

Therefore, the response time is determined by the proximity of the firefighters to the station and their availability. Over the years many towns have grown to a size that has mandated the conversion from a call department to a paid department.

A major concern is the so-called 'bedroom community' which has many available personnel at night and on the weekends, but very few during the day, since most of the members work out-of-town. A fire chief once told me that he had four firefighters show up at a house fire in the afternoon, but had twenty arrive for an auto fire at midnight. Full time firefighters are needed so that a minimal number of firefighters are on duty ready for an immediate response. This manning system, albeit rudimentary, still doesn't consider a working fire where many more firefighters will be needed.

The fire department with a limited number of on-duty firefighters causes a town to rely heavily on mutual aid. Mutual aid is an agreement with the bordering towns so that each town responds to the other's needs for manpower and equipment. Mutual aid was devised in the 19th century to prevent conflagrations. Today it is used on a daily basis.

The biggest problem with a fire department having only two or three members on duty is that the ambulance is usually run by the fire department and consequently the personnel may be tied up at a medical transport when the fire call comes in. Since the on-duty members are tied up at a hospital which may be a considerable distance away or in another town, the call firefighters are relied upon in the absence of on-duty personnel.

I have had discussions with fire chiefs in this type of fire department whereby the chief insists that he has a full time fire department when in reality what he has is a full time ambulance service which responds to fire calls when available.

So you can see that each community has factors that affect the response time to fires and other emergencies. The fire department is usually a well-respected organization, however few appreciate its cost or existence until the fire department is needed at *their* house.

I have given you an overview about the types of fire departments so that the time frame of the response can be understood. It has always been said that minutes count when a fire is in its incipiency, but this is also true for medical emergencies. When the brain goes without oxygen for four minutes, the chance for survival is greatly reduced or there may be no chance at all for survival.

♪♪♪♫

Let's return to the subject of the fire department's arrival at an emergency scene. "Organized confusion" is the term usually given to the chaotic looking dispersal of firefighters upon their arrival.

The first engine company on the scene has the job of getting water to the seat of the fire in anticipation of keeping the fire contained to the area of origin. When a fire is attacked quickly and efficiently it is usually done with few or no problems. However, throw in a few problems and the situation goes from bad to worse in minutes, if not seconds.

Parked cars, locked doors, multiple floors to ascend, no access to windows or the concern for life safety can quickly turn a routine operation into a dilemma. This adds the need for more manpower and/or equipment.

No hydrants, limited hydrants, long driveways, snow, fog, rain, and just the darkness of the nighttime are all factors to consider when a fire occurs.

Familiarity with the neighborhood is important. Is it a multi-family house or a small one story bungalow.

Sometimes the extent of the fire is so advanced upon the arrival of the fire department that the primary goal is to prevent the fire from spreading to other homes or structures.

♪♪♪

Let's take the 'normal' arrival at a fire scene with the 'normal' situations encountered. In Boston we attack a fire with a large number of firefighters in an attempt to 'keep it small'. Three engines, two ladders, a rescue company and a district chief respond to every report of a structure fire. Each company has four members assigned. In the downtown area there is also a tower ladder assigned with a deputy fire chief too. Every structure fire sees the dispatch of a RIT company. This is a fire company which stands by with only one assignment: rescue of a downed firefighter should such an event occur.

Without delay, the first engine company to arrive runs an attack line to the front door and the first arriving ladder company positions the aerial ladder to the roof. This is done without orders from Command or words spoken. Both of these operations may be adjusted depending on the location of the fire or the anticipation of rescues being made. While the first due engine and ladder are engaged in their duties, the balance of the assignment is following department protocol upon their arrival.

The second and third due engines are taking a position at a hydrant. All three engine companies on the first alarm should be on their own hydrant under normal circumstances. The second arriving ladder company will attempt to take the rear of the building and, if it is not possible, position the ladder truck at a neighboring building. The second engine company will probably be directed to run a line to the floor above the fire.

As the officer and two firefighters from the first arriving engine company bring the attack line to the front door, the pump operator secures a water supply and charges the attack line.

The officer of the first ladder company and the 'open up' firefighter go to the door and, if necessary, force entry to prepare access for the engine company. The chauffeur of the ladder company is positioning the aerial ladder to the roof and the 'roof man' is preparing to go to the roof to survey the situation and, if necessary, ventilate.

Locked doors cause only a minimal delay, however barricaded doors and barred windows are a serious detriment to life safety. People barricade doors and bar windows to deter burglars and thieves from gaining entry into the home, but these same devices also deter the firefighters from entering and the occupants from escaping.

The key word to focus on here is *access*. When this access is impeded, the end result is a delay, which causes the fire to grow exponentially before water is applied.

A rapid response to the scene can be delayed by parked cars on the corners. Parked cars on hydrants can delay securing a water supply. Also parked cars can prohibit the jacking system of a ladder truck from being properly deployed.

Boston and the surrounding communities have an abundance of three-deckers. A three-decker is a three story wood framed building with similar apartments on each floor. The bedrooms, bathrooms, and kitchens on each floor are stacked above each other. Pipe chases run from the cellar to the top floor. These chases contain all of the piping, gas and plumbing, electrical wiring. They create an express route for the heat, smoke and fire to travel vertically.

When the fire is encountered on the first floor, a main concern to the firefighters is the extension of the fire up the unenclosed staircase. As stated earlier heat, smoke and gases tend to rise. When the fire is on the upper floors, the heat and gases have nowhere to go, so they bank down at the ceiling and redeploy to the lower floors. This, added to the extra time for the firefighters to ascend to the upper floors with the hose line, can cause delays also.

The roof firefighter from the first arriving ladder company goes to the roof and surveys the situation. What is he looking for? First, the softness or sponginess of the roof is a major concern. This would signify that the fire has gained considerable headway under the roof and collapse could very well be an issue.

If the roof seems secure, the next question is 'where is the fire concentrated'. Smoke emanating from windows may show the area of fire involvement. The bubbling of tar on a roof or even the sound of the fire burning below is extremely important.

A roof firefighter may be able to lean over the edge of the roof and, using a long handled tool, be able to break the top floor windows for immediate ventilation. If the fire is determined to be on the top floor, then vertical ventilation will be necessary. The first mode of gaining this objective is to take advantage of natural systems such as roof bulkhead doors, skylights, or other man-made objects found on a roof.

When necessary, preparation should begin on the roof hole. A roof hole never should be put in a roof at a distance from the fire. It is absolutely necessary to position the hole over the fire area. Cutting the hole with a power saw is the easiest way to make this opening, however the use of an axe is sometimes the chosen method.

What is accomplished by all of this ventilation? The heat, toxic gases and smoke are given a route to the atmosphere where they can no longer harm the occupants or the firefighters.

The hose line that was taken to the fire floor by the engine company is used to apply water to the fire through a 'fog' pattern. What does this tend to do? The fog pattern pushes the heat, smoke, and gases ahead of the water, through the ventilation opening, safely to the outside. The hose line can now continue to be advanced and also allow rescues to be made.

When ventilation has not been accomplished yet, the smoke, heat and gases hit the back wall and rapidly return in the direction of the firefighters on the hose line because this is most likely the only opening into the fire area. Hopefully the attack team is crouched low enough so the aforementioned products of combustion travel over their heads.

The advancement of the first engine company's attack line needs to be closely monitored and in synchronization with the ventilation efforts of the ladder company.

By describing the actions of the first due fire companies, I hope to have given you a clarification into why all of this confusion is happening. Remember that each firefighter is wearing about 45 pounds of protective equipment on their person while climbing stairs, advancing hose lines, climbing ladders and attacking the fire. In the summertime when everybody else is undressing, firefighters still have to gear up for a fire.

CHAPTER 2

Ten Firefighting Myths

Ten firefighting myths that I have heard over my forty years:

1. Firefighters like to break windows and chop holes in roofs

2. Firefighters drive like crazy, maybe 50 to 60 mph going to fires.

3. Firefighters breathe oxygen when they go into fire buildings.

4. Firefighters sit around and do nothing all day.

5. Firefighters eat supper on the city's dime.

6. Firefighters use the city's vehicles to shop for lunch or dinner.

7. The fire department is a great job for those with only a high school diploma.

8. Firefighters make a ton of money.

9. Firefighters sleep on the job.

10. It's raining so there will be no fires today.

Myth Number One

Firefighters like to break windows and chop holes in roofs.

Firefighters open windows when they are able to do so. Holes in roofs are made when necessary. When a firefighter is forced to crawl on his/her knees or bellies, standing up to open windows is not an option. Windows can be quickly broken with a tool, fire helmet or a stream of water. Hence, firefighters do not enjoy breaking windows, but do so in attempt to quickly extinguish the fire with minimal damage.

Some fire chiefs feel that a roof hole is expensive to repair or replace. Repairing a roof hole is a lot cheaper than replacing the entire top floor and its possessions. I consider it an inept decision not to ventilate the roof when deemed necessary.

Remember that the heat in a fully involved fire area can reach temperatures of 1100 to 1400 degrees at the ceiling. This temperature coupled with the smoke that has completely obliterated firefighters' vision mandates that they crawl along floors for safety and survival.

An important thought to remember is that a hole in the roof serves a very important purpose: the evacuation of smoke, heat and fire gases. That hole is never to be used for the application of water into the fire from a heavy stream appliance such as a deck gun or ladder pipe.

I have witnessed many a building lost by the foolhardy decision to improperly order firefighters to play water into a roof hole. This action spread the fire throughout the building's interior into rooms where it previously never had a desire to go. This unintentional misdirection of fire shows the incident commander that this was a regrettable decision.

Myth Number Two

Firefighters drive like crazy, maybe fifty to sixty miles per hour going to fires.

If you are standing on the curb at a busy intersection and a car goes by driving at 40 mph, you probably wouldn't even pay attention to it. Along comes a big, red (at least I hope it is red) fire engine or maybe a ladder truck which comes along driving at 30 mph. It probable has its siren operating and maybe even the air horn is blasting a warning to traffic and pedestrians alike.

"Wow, did you see that fire truck fly by?" says one lady to her husband. Their two children wave to the firefighters inside and the firefighters wave back. They are donning their protective gear, anticipating a true emergency at their destination.

Perhaps it isn't even going 30 mph, but even slower. The size of the monster coupled with the noise certainly makes it appear to the un-trained eye that the fire apparatus is 'flying'. My forty years of either driving or riding in the front seat can testify that under most circum-stances that big red fire truck will rarely ever exceed 30-35 mph with-in the city.

This doesn't mean that it won't or can't exceed that speed. However a professional, prudent firefighter knows that stopping that twenty-ton vehicle (It carries 750 gallons of water and myriads of other equip-ment) is going to be a chore, at best.

The safety of the pedestrians and that of the occupants of the other vehicles on the road is paramount. Couple that with the fact that we are useless to our citizens if we never make it to an emergency be-cause of involvement in a motor vehicle accident. These facts make it mandatory that speed be kept under control and the braking ability be maintained while responding to each and every incident.

One thing that I explain to visitors and firefighters from other fire departments is that in the downtown area, pedestrians are our biggest nightmare. The rush to get to work on time will cause an otherwise safety minded worker to figure that they have time to run across the street in front of us as we respond through the crowded streets of downtown Boston.

Let's take the single most hazardous obstacle to pedestrian safety since the invention of sneakers, the cell phone. People talking on cell phones with the phone glued to their ear, will walk right out between parked cars or step off the curb absolutely oblivious to the impending collision with, not just a piece of fire apparatus, but with any vehicle on the road.

The state law says that when a driver is approached by an emergency vehicle with its warning lights and sirens operating, the driver of said vehicle must pull over to the right and stop until it is safe to proceed. In the City of Boston, 60% of the drivers apparently missed that question when they got their license and another 30% feel that stopping to the left is just as good as pulling over to the right.

Boston seems to be the jaywalking capital of the world, but when you couple that with the omnipresent hazard, the bicycle messenger, you need to focus your complete attention to driving every time you venture onto the roadways of the city proper. One thing the bike messenger has in his/her repertoire is that they must have been trained by either Mario Andretti or the Japanese Kamikaze pilots of World War II.

Another fact of life in the city is that if you come upon 15 traffic signals in your commute, you will arrive at 9 of them while red, 4 turning yellow and perhaps 2 of them momentarily still green.

So you see, it is not only unlikely that the big red fire engine is speeding, but downright near impossible.

Myth Number Three

Myth number three is that most people think that firefighters are breathing oxygen when they don their air masks before entering a fire building.

The media, both in print and on television, constantly reports this incorrect fact, perpetuating this myth.

The media commits an injustice to the viewing public, which I refer to as compromising the believability factor. When a story is related on the local news station or in the newspaper and an incorrect address is used or improper localized terms are used it reaffirms to the public that the newscasters and reporters are not from this area.

When a newscaster is thought to be from out of town, the public doubts that they know what they are talking about or that they share the same concerns. People like to feel as though their local media are familiar with the area and with the situations surrounding local residents.

Some of these common breaches of faith are the use of wrong addresses such as Warren Street being referred to as Warren Avenue or any other thoroughfare being tagged with the wrong suffix.

Another concern is local terms not being properly applied. One of my pet peeves is the term 'triple-decker'. Anyone who grew up in Boston or lived most of their life in Boston or the surrounding cities knows that those three story wood frame buildings are three-deckers and not the incorrect term, triple- decker. I usually think of a triple decker as a huge sandwich served in a delicatessen.

Now this may not seem important to you, however if a local term is incorrectly used over and over, it destroys the 'believability factor'.

While we are on the subject of the media, another term that they have begun using is our endearing term 'Jake'. This is a common name for a firefighter that the members of fire departments have used for many years. It is *our* term and the members of the media have no right to take it upon themselves to use it.

Hardly a day goes by lately that a newspaper does not contain the word. In reality, the reason they use it is because on convenience. It is a lot shorter and easier to fit into a headline than 'firefighter'. Attention media reporters and editors: "Stop using our phrase!" We don't refer to you by your pet names, whatever they are. It took twenty five years to get you people to stop calling us firemen. We are firefighters and the term firefighter is non-gender binding. It also more accurately describes our mission.

I'm sorry if I have once again drifted off topic. I will now get back to the myth at hand: air masks, not oxygen masks.

In the hospital or in an ambulance you might have an oxygen mask applied to increase the oxygen flow to your blood. People incorrectly assume that oxygen is flammable. This assumption is exacerbated by the fact that you constantly see 'No Smoking' signs around the use of oxygen. While pure oxygen itself is not an explosion hazard, it is dangerous since open flames in its presence will cause rapid and intense burning. Oxygen will not explode, however it will intensify the burning rate of a fire when pure oxygen is present.

As you can now understand, even if oxygen was needed to breathe, it would be extremely dangerous to a firefighter to have pure oxygen readily available in a hazardous atmosphere.

So what is it that our firefighters are breathing when they enter a fire building wearing those units strapped to their backs with those face pieces attached to their heads and faces. It is simply compressed air, the common everyday air that you and I breathe. It is the common air containing about 79% nitrogen and 20% oxygen plus trace quantities of other gaseous products.

This air is contained in the air bottles under pressure. In the commonly referred to one-half hour cylinder, a firefighter can expect to get about 18 to 20 minutes of work time. You might wonder why it is called a half hour bottle if only 18 to 20 minutes is the average work time. These times are obtained by wearing the air mask with a half hour cylinder attached while sitting or standing at rest. Remember that a firefighter is working while wearing it. He or she may be climbing stairs, crawling down hallways, operating a hose line, opening up a roof, or doing a search and rescue operation. All of these aforementioned activities are not done at rest, of course, and the adrenalin is usually pumping while the firefighter performs them.

Today firefighters have the ability to choose between so-called half-hour bottles, three-quarter hour bottles and one-hour bottles. None of these will last for the time suggested.

So you might ask, "Why not use a one hour bottle if you can stay in the fire building longer without having to exit to change cylinders". The answer is weight; the weight of the cylinder is greater since the size of the cylinder is larger to contain a greater amount of compressed air to last for a longer time period.

In Boston, firefighters are compelled by the Standard Operating Guidelines to use one-hour cylinders in their air masks when fighting fires in subway fires, in sub-basement fires or when on board ships where a fire is suspected or visible. They may also wear the one-hour cylinders at any other time that they may choose.

꜒꜒꜒

Hopefully, this chapter provides some insight into the use of air masks and the difference between air and oxygen. I have used the term air mask in this chapter since that is the term we use in the Boston Fire Department. Many fire departments use the term SCBA (Self-contained breathing apparatus). This is the proper manufacturer's term for these breathing units, however 'air masks' or just 'masks' is how firefighters most commonly refer to them.

Myth Number Four

<u>Firefighters sit around and do nothing all day waiting for the next fire.</u>

The day shift begins at 0800, (That's 8:00 in the morning for you non-military types), although most are in the firehouse between 0700 and 0730.

The day begins with the night shift bringing the oncoming day shift up to speed with whatever may have occurred in the previous 24 hours.

Although it may seem to the untrained eye that these firefighters are sitting in the firehouse kitchen drinking coffee, what is actually happening is the sharing of experiences to increase the efficiency of the firefighters. Now many of our own are reading this and are thinking, "Wow, is he full of horseshit!" One must realize that the discussion of what went right or what may have not have worked out for the best is actually a learning experience.

Discussion of firefighting actions, training sessions, or whatever else may have occurred in the preceding tour of duty is absorbed whether you realize it or not. At the next fire where similar circumstances dictate actions, you may suddenly remember the discussion you had at the kitchen table three or four days, months, or even years ago.

Remember, that even the most disinterested individual will absorb some information even if they do not intend to digest it. Many times, experiences have shown me that firefighters who sit around and appear content with inactivity suddenly become motivated firefighters when the house alarm goes off.

As far as training sessions go, a discussion of the previous day's training will enable a firefighter to perhaps do a more efficient job, since inaccuracies or inefficiencies may be pointed out during these morning BS sessions.

〜〜〜〜

At 0830 the daily housework chores begin. The company officers start their paperwork and the chief officers check into the day's schedule to make sure that everything is in order.

The firefighters clean the kitchen, and sweep and mop the floors because, unlike every other job, there are no custodians to perform these tasks. Depending upon the day of the week, the windows might need to be washed, the brass polished, or the kitchen refrigerators and stoves may need to be emptied and scoured.

Then the process moves to the apparatus floor where the equipment and tools on every company must be started, operated, cleaned, checked, and oiled. Then the engines and ladders, towers and chiefs' vehicles must be washed. This happens daily and must be done by the firefighters because, unlike the police who take their vehicles to the car wash, it is expected of the on-duty crews. After these events, then the apparatus must be fueled and the engine oil and transmission fluid checked.

An engine company has a water tank which must also be inspected to assure that it is full of water and ready for the next alarm.

Years ago these 'booster' tanks had a maximum of 125 gallons which, over the years, was increased to 500 gallons. Most new pumpers come from the factory with a tank having a capacity of 750 gallons of water today.

This brings us to the time for the daily drill schedule to kick in. For some companies it means traveling to the fire academy for monthly, semi-annual or annual drills. For others these drills take place in the fire station and for still some others the drills are held at the classrooms at Fire Headquarters. These drills may be to update skills involving

First Responder medical situations, use of the Semi-automatic external defibrillator (SAED), CPR or bio-health hazards, which may be encountered at any emergency.

Technical rescue companies may be involved in annual skills updating in accordance with any of the technical rescue categories such as trench rescue, confined space rescue, building collapse rescue, tunnel rescue, patient packaging or rope rescue.

For some companies the training might be 'back to basics' training involving first due company hose and ladder evolutions. It may be fit testing of the air mask face pieces or completion of the 'maze' training. Face pieces for the air masks must be tested annually so that it can be determined whether or not the proper seal can be attained so that toxic gases and smoke particles will not enter the respiratory system of the firefighter while wearing these life sustaining devices.

The maze is a program whereby a firefighter is entered into an area intended to simulate situations that a firefighter may encounter when in a fire building. The firefighter is protected by all of the protective gear assigned to him/her. A face piece is donned which has been covered so that no visibility is available. This simulates a most hazardous fire scenario and the firefighter has to find his or her way out of the maze using skills learned from their training and personal experiences.

Firefighters in the burn building, which is a training building in which fires may be set to simulate the 'real world' situations facing firefighters, may be called upon to run a hose line or to rescue a distressed person, simulated by the use of a mannequin. Once again, skills are entertained which have been learned by training and life experiences.

An important tool which firefighters train with in the burn building is the Thermal Imaging Camera. This tool shows firefighters, through the temperature differential, the location of a person in the smoke filled area or perhaps the location of the fire when it cannot be seen by the human eye.

These are some of the training sessions to which your firefighters are dispatched to on a regular schedule to sharpen skills so that the public can have a reasonable expectation of the response of well-trained, capable firefighters in case of an emergency. I don't think that the average taxpayer ever really knows how much training and equipment is necessary for the proper protection of the citizenry.

Don't forget that during all of this daily routine, the average fire company probably has had two or three runs (fire or medical calls).

This probably brings us up to lunchtime. While returning from a run or drill, the company might stop at a sandwich shop or restaurant to pick up sandwiches or some other take-out.

Remember this!! This is the only job that I know of that does not have a specific lunch break. It is eat when you can or perhaps, chomp on a sandwich between calls. We are normal human beings and need to eat to survive just like every taxpayer that we protect.

⌒⌒⌒⌒

OK, lunch is finally over. Today we had to leave our lunch on the table twice for a response. The second time we were tied up for 45 minutes.

It is now 1340 hours. The officer is called to the main floor because a group of children from the neighborhood preschool have stopped in for a tour. The captain assigns two of the firefighters to give the tour and to answer the numerous and entertaining questions that the youngsters have. One of the single guys later thanks the captain for choosing him since he found out that one of the preschool teachers was single, gorgeous and available.

Usually, after the attendance of a school-aged group, a thank you is delivered to the firehouse from the children. They are always made in the kids own individual handwriting and accompanied by pictures that they have drawn from their experiences which they learned from their trip to the firehouse. Their imagination of the tasks that we perform is incredible and these messages of thanks stay posted on the bulletin board for months.

Sometimes it a picture of the firemen washing the apparatus, or it may be a fire with a hose line trained on the fire building or it may be a picture of the firehouse mascot, be it a dog or cat, that they enjoyed seeing during their visit.

One thing I have always noticed is that, with very few exceptions, all children who visit the firehouse want to be a firefighter when they grow up.

This brings us to the late afternoon preparation of the evening meal. Meals have to be planned in advance because one or two runs will delay supper until 2000 hours or later. Rarely is a meal completed without an interruption for some type of emergency. By the way, no one usually complains since everyone is aware that this is a side effect of the job and career we have chosen.

On a rare occasion, supper will be so destroyed after reheating two or three times that the whole thing gets chucked into the trash and on the next run we have to stop for pizza. Remembering once again, there is no designated supper hour either.

Oh and remember someone has to feed the cat!

Tucked into the day's activities are the numerous telephone calls for information on a previous day's activities, setting up a paid detail for a construction site or for a place of assembly so that the safety of the general public is ensured. The company strengths for the next day have to be balanced. This may involve hiring a member for an overtime shift or detailing a firefighter from one firehouse to another.

A contractor or a building representative may stop by to speak with the chief or the company officer.

Maybe around 9 pm (2100) things settle down enough so that you might have time to read department emails, relay information from the daily orders to the personnel or hold a company drill in the television room. Perhaps a video will be shown on a new tool or a more efficient way to perform a task.

Even though firehouses still have beds so that the members might rest between alarms, don't ever call it a night's sleep because that just doesn't happen.

That's what we do when the public, and the political hacks, think we are just hanging around doing nothing. As we discuss this myth let me delve further into the training aspect of the job. We don't get to be as good as we are without training.

Training has been the subject of this chapter. While it has often been stated that firefighters are having fewer fires these days, there are other skills needed to be learned. Technical skills for safety or rescue for both the firefighters and the public that they serve are constantly being reviewed.

It is true that fires are down and the fires are down for various reasons. The first is probably the fact that the housing market has eliminated the vacant buildings that we so commonly responded to twenty, thirty, forty years ago. These buildings are far more valuable than they once were. An apartment in a three-decker, which probably commanded rent of about $100 a month forty years ago, now rents for $800 to $1200 or more depending upon its location.

A second reason would be that arson is a problem area where great strides have been made. In the 1960s an arsonist did not have much worry about apprehension where today's Fire Investigation Unit is more high tech, better trained and, seemingly, more motivated than in the past.

Thirdly, smoke detectors are bringing the fire department to the scene of an impending fire more quickly than ever before. Years ago a fire might have smoldered for hours before detection, where with the presence of a smoke detector, the fire is noticed sooner today. Smoke detectors work even when nobody is home or present in the workplace.

There are two types of smoke detectors on the market today; ionization and photoelectric. Deputy Fire Chief Joseph (Jay) Fleming of the Boston Fire Department has done thousands of hours of research on the matter and has become an expert in the field. Smoke detector manufacturers dread his appearance at a conference or seminar where he speaks on the inadequacies of ionization type detectors. These detectors are activated by the presence of a fire as opposed to photo-electric detectors, which detect smoldering fires in their incipiency.

Remember that smoke detectors are cheap insurance that your family will be protected should a fire occur in your home, but the proper detector is a primary factor in that safety. No smoke detector should ever have the battery removed for any reason. This action of battery removal completely invalidates the sense of safety that is present in your home.

Along with smoke detectors we have encountered another problem.

·oblem is the tremendous increase in fire department responses to automatic fire alarms in buildings, the activation of a smoke detector that occurs for a non-fire reason. Naturally the fire department has no way of knowing whether a true emergency exists so their response is the same to every call.

Occupants of buildings that have repeated alarms for non-fire causes become lackadaisical and frequently pay no more attention to fire alarms in their buildings than they do of the sirens that they hear in the city on a daily basis.

So this becomes a two-fold problem area. First the fire department responds needlessly presenting a danger of more emergency vehicles on the streets and secondly; the benefit of an early warning system for a hazard in a building is ignored by those who hear the warning once or twice a week.

How many times do we have to respond to an area of a building where the eating facilities are located and find that a bag of microwave popcorn has been opened right underneath a smoke detector? The public should be cognizant of the presence of the smoke detectors and realize that this is not an accepted practice.

When smoking was still considered acceptable in buildings response to elevator lobby smoke detectors was a common occurrence since people lit their cigarettes, cigars, or pipes while waiting for an elevator.

Another common run for us is to the homes of people who return home late at night hungry. While some of these incidents involve inebriated folks, many are just simply tired people who put something on the stove or in the oven and then fall fast asleep. While they are in dreamland, the smoke detector is still at work. The cooking becomes burning and the device then detects the burning. The device summons the fire department and then, presto, we arrive to the obvious odor of food burning on the stove.

Occasionally the detector is not hard-wired and the high-pitched sound of the alarm causes another occupant to call the fire department. In this case we arrive at the location and must try to awaken the occupant of the offending apartment or, if that is not successful, then a forcible entry is made.

Sometimes a detector is either not present or has had the battery removed. Now it is the odor of the burning food which becomes the cause for alarm. The call for a fire comes from a neighbor and once again the fire department is on the scene in a matter of minutes. Not knowing which unit the burning odor is coming from, a search of the entire building is undertaken until we determine that we have found the guilty apartment. Many times the occupant/chef has left the building not realizing that the stove was still on.

Frequently the smoldering, burning food in the pan actually ignites and spreads by convection to the surrounding materials in the kitchen and an actual fire occurs. A potholder or dishtowel may be too close to the stove. Perhaps it is the curtain or some other flammable object that becomes ignited. Many times this food on the stove incident has spread beyond the stove and a significant fire is encountered.

᛭᛭᛭

Now that we have discussed the reasons that fires may be down let's get back to training.

The fire department trains on many subjects. Some of these are fire attack, emergency medical calls, computer training, fire reports, self-contained breathing apparatus, search and rescue, elevator accidents, auto accident extrication.

We also have technical rescue teams that train on a variety of tech rescues such as building collapse, rope rescues, trench rescue, confined space incidents, high angle rescue, below grade rescue, water incidents, tunnel rescue.

Any of these disciplines involve time and effort for a safe and successful outcome. Many of the aforementioned rescue responses are met upon our arrival with well-intentioned rescuers entering hazardous areas since they have no training in the hazards involved. Occasionally these rescuers become victims themselves and double or triple our problems.

Fire department training with the MBTA involves a wide area of subjects. Some of which are jacking trains or buses, ventilating stations of the smoke which may be produced in a fire situation, extinguishment of fires in tunnels, trains, or buses. We learn the hazards of operating at a bus incident with compressed natural gas buses or 600 volt electrical hazards with trains or trolleys.

Firefighters participate in pre-fire planning in buildings which have been recently completed, under construction, under renovation or perhaps have been around for many years.

Elevators which have a different technology that the usual such as the double decked elevators at the John Hancock tower on Clarendon Street in the Back Bay or the smart elevators at 1 Federal Street, Downtown.

The double decked elevators at the Hancock building open on two different neighboring floors at the same time. These elevators require elaborate training for firefighting personnel to ensure that no one is in either car prior to firefighting operations.

The smart elevators at One Federal Street encompass an operation that takes the rider to one floor and then becomes available to take another rider to his or her floor. These elevators do not make stops at any floors other than the destination floor entered. Instead of pressing an up or down call button, a rider enters his or her intended floor number at the call station. You are then told which elevator is yours and the floor of destination is express. No stops are made during the trip to your floor.

Hazards in buildings are addressed in training. Many buildings have hazards which are unique to the procedures undertaken in this manufacturing or assembly process.

Boston has numerous tunnels and roadways, most of which are monitored by cameras located at the OCC (Operations Control Center) of the Massachusetts Turnpike Authority headquarters building in South Boston. Drills are held at this location so that the firefighters become familiar with the systems employed. Some of these systems involve fire protection, communication, roadway access, ventilation systems, etc.

Rail yards contain many hazards, as do chemical plants. The Brighton section of the city contains both of these hazards.

Hospitals and schools have many areas of concern such as laboratories and egress systems.

Theaters, night clubs and other places of assembly, including some concert venues, usually have a large audience unfamiliar with egress points.

Hotels contain hundreds of rooms or suites, and maybe conference rooms and banquet facilities occupied by thousands of people. Most of these people have never been in this particular environment before and will be here for only this one event.

Other trainings that occur on a daily basis are computer training and refreshers, incident reporting, training on a new or improved piece of equipment, protective gear or communication device.

Emergency medical training subjects may be first responder information updates, recent encountered illnesses, SAED (Semi-automated emergency device) operations, epi-pens, health protection for the firefighters, etc.

The fire department has been criticized by the detractors over the years as unnecessary, undertrained responders. Well we have thirty three fire stations spread throughout the city, so it is fairly common knowledge that we will have emergency personnel on the scene within four minutes if necessary.

As far as undertrained, our members have certified training in CPR, SAED, many are EMTs (with no additional compensation), Paramedics (with no additional compensation, nor recognition), and a few are nurses. Every firefighter receives first-responder training at least semi-annually and by law have to be involved even when bystanders do not want to be.

Every year we have members of the fire department who are commended for taking action at an incident while off duty and many more that perform actions when off duty, but are not recognized. Our firefighters do not stand around and wait for this recognition, but act when the need is such for any action being taken.

Earlier I mentioned the detractors. You may be wondering who this group is. Let me elaborate. It is the politicians who see us as a burden. It is the so-called experts who chair positions in groups who champion their causes of overseeing the city's business interests, such as the Boston Municipal Research Bureau and the Boston Finance Commission.

It is members of ambulance services who have not been able to attain a position on the fire department and envy the firefighters for each and every accomplishment that we have succeeded in attaining. Nobody gives us any of our benefits. Our union has to fight for every benefit we have ever worked tirelessly to receive.

Our union's contract has been tried and tested in the media by City Hall recently. No other union's contract has, just the firefighters. Why you might ask? Is it because the firefighters stand up to a mayor who is too thin-skinned to be a politician? He doesn't realize that this is business and his is an ego the size of no other politician in recent memory.

The City of Boston now has a new and refreshing administration in City Hall. Mayor Marty Walsh has taken over the reins and has already created a more professional attitude when the city and the unions go to the bargaining table. Thank you, Mayor Marty.

The other haters are the bloggers who hide behind the nameless, face-less blogs that generate hate and venom. They do not have the balls to sign their real name or to come forward and make their sentiments known in public. They sit at home in the safety of anonymity at their computers acting bravely, but in reality in cowardice.

I would never reply to these people since that reaction is what they are attempting to garner. This is the orgasm of their twisted sexual deviance that they engage in on a daily occurrence. Come on! Come forward!! Identify your cowardly face so that we can know our enemies.

A certain member of the BPPA (Area A) kicks our balls off and a certain member of Boston EMS (A1) likewise kicks our balls off. Whatever happened to 'Brotherhood"? The only positive thing I can say is that these "brothers' at least have the balls to sign their names to their letters of hate, unlike the bloggers.

When has Local 718 ever knocked any other unions when they were down? I think the answer is 'Never'.

Myth Number Five

Firefighters eat their meals on the city's dime.

While we have discussed food and lunch breaks in the previous myth, I have to tell you about the number of times that I have been asked if the city supplies us with our food. I can't believe that there are some people out there who actually think this.

I'll tell you what the city does supply us with. They supply us with the stove, the refrigerator, water and toilet paper. They supply us with minimal supplies for cleaning the firehouse we call our second home, but they expect it to be cleaned daily.

They do **not** supply us with food, coffee, televisions, gymnasium equipment, paper towels, pots, pans, dishes, or silverware. Most of the furniture that we have in the firehouse has been procured by begging from an office building or a school which may be fortunate enough to receive new furniture and then the firefighters eye their old junk as being newer and more comfortable for us. Some of the guys whose families are buying a new couch or recliner ask us if we are interested in taking the old one.

Occasionally the group in the firehouse chips in to buy a new television or a new recliner. Remember to always buy the best since our stuff gets a lot of hard use.

Only in recent years has the City supplied us with window washing materials or soap and wax for the fire apparatus.

We buy our own washing machines and dryers, detergent and other odds and ends, which make life a little easier. We paint our own walls and wash and wax our own floors. (Remember, no janitors).

We decorate our walls with photos, flags, and other paraphernalia, which we purchase because we have pride in the fire service and in our firehouse in particular.

Oh, I almost forgot about the exterior of the firehouse. We mow our own grass; we shovel our snow and clean up outside the firehouse for the safety and convenience of the public.

About every fifteen years we receive a new fire engine, which we take care of like it is our own because we know that we will be riding on it for the next 15 years.

Myth Number Six

We use the city's vehicles to pick up lunch and dinner.

While I am addressing this as a myth, it really is an actuality. We are allowed to stop at the store or sandwich shop to pick up our lunch or shop for our supper. While we may be thought of by some as super-human, firefighters have to eat for nourishment just like every other human being.

Occasionally one of our citizens, or more likely a non-citizen, makes a snide remark about our stopping with the fire engine for lunch pick-up. They need to be reminded that we are available by radio for the next alarm and, very frequently, have to leave to respond to an alarm before our order is ready for the checkout to respond. I wonder if that inconsiderate person has ever had to leave his or her meal to run out to help someone in need of assistance.

Once again, how many people are expected to go to work and not stop for lunch or dinner? We cannot send someone out for our meals, so we stop when returning to the firehouse from a call or a drill. We don't unnecessarily use the city's fuel and we are always ready to respond by radio which we very often do.

Frequently, while we are out, we may perform a public service such as giving directions to an out-of-towner, answer questions about our fire apparatus or protective gear, or perhaps allow a visitor to photograph the firefighters as a memory of their trip to Boston. Very frequently the visitor likes to have their picture taken in front of the fire engine and usually requests some of the members to join them in the photo.

Never for a moment does this delay our response to an emergency. In actuality we are already dressed and ready to go and frequently in the vicinity of the alarm.

Myth Number Seven

The fire department is a great job for those who have only a high school diploma.

Gone are the days when most firefighters had only a high school education. Many firefighters, me included, continue their education and so many today have Associates' degrees, Bachelors' degrees and even masters degrees. Some have studied fire science, but some also have degrees in education or nursing.

In our daily lambasting, which we are subject to lately from both the previous mayor and the media, our firefighters always attempt to please the citizenry with a helping hand. It doesn't matter if it is helping a lady with a baby stroller go up or down some stairs, or assisting a motorist who has inadvertently locked their keys in the car. The guys are glad to help out. The usual explanation for going out of their way to assist someone is, "I would like to think someone would do the same for my wife or kids".

Many neighborhood firehouses will put air in a tire for a local kid with a bicycle since the corner gas station charges now for air. Many a flat tire has been fixed for a child and many more flat tires on a car have been changed for a 'damsel in distress.'

Oftentimes a call goes out over the public address system in the firehouse, "Anyone got jumper cables?" "Does anyone have this tool or that tool?" Never does a call for assistance go unheeded by the firemen at the local firehouse. Oh, by the way, monetary rewards are never accepted.

If you need directions to a street, to a restaurant, to a theater, a school or a hospital, you can get any of the aforementioned at the firehouse.

It may be a drink of water in the summertime or perhaps a visit to the restroom. We are there to help out!

Many a car has broken down outside. If we cannot get it running, then you are welcome to sit inside while you wait for AAA. Perhaps you will be offered a cup of firehouse coffee, if you dare.

A few years back an out-of-town mayor from Ireland had his rented electric wheelchair break down three blocks from the hotel in which he was staying. Guess who made sure that he got back to his hotel safely?

Out-of-towners strolling by with their youngsters peering in through the overhead doors are met with a "Come on in and show the kids the fire engines".

"Want to sit on the fire engine?" is almost always met with a "Sure!" A kid wanting to see a firefighter slide the pole will be obliged because we have all been there at a time in our own lives.

In spite of all of our intentions to please the public, we receive gritty comments from an occasional person who perhaps believes all of the bullshit that he or she reads in the Boston Globe about firefighters. The Boston Globe, the local newspaper that honors a pledge to report nothing positive about the Boston Fire Department. Only negatives!

We had a mayor for twenty years who took everything personally. This was same mayor who allowed city hall leak out every facet of the firefighter's union contract negotiations to the press, whether true or not. Constant exaggeration of facts and figures, attempted intimidation of our members and the selected brown outs of fire companies in the neighborhoods. At the risk of harm to the citizenry, he thinks he is hurting us by not filling in for sick members. I guess no one at city hall ever got sick.

Over the recent couple of years, seven or so members have been accused or disciplined of wrongdoing. None of these alleged acts have ever been sanctioned by the membership or the local union. These seven members of a 1400 plus member fire department represent, by my calculation, about one half of one percent of the membership. Not to trivialize any of their issues, but no murders, rapes nor federal crimes, such as bank robberies were committed. I challenge any organization or workforce to boast that they have a lesser number than that of members who have screwed up.

Every occupation has its share of employees dealing with demons. We handle our own through our Employee Assistance Program and give them an opportunity to make amends and straighten out their lives.

As a fire officer in charge of a fire company, I have never and would never allow an individual to work while impaired by any substance. Given this statement, in twenty-five years as an officer, I have never had to send anyone home nor disallowed him or her to work because of suspected impairment. This doesn't mean that it doesn't ever happen, but my point here is that I personally have never encountered it.

Drug testing. The media, at the behest of the mayor, reports that the firefighters' union balks at attempts to implement drug testing. What is never refuted is the fact that the fire department has drug testing in place and has had it in place for years, so many years, in fact, that I can't remember when it came about.

What is different from our drug testing and the drug testing that the city demands, is that our testing is done when cause warrants. Anytime a company officer or chief officer feels that a firefighter's performance or lack thereof suggests possible impairment that individual is referred to a drug testing facility immediately.

The city wants random drug testing. Other agencies in the city have the current 'random' testing in place now whereby random means within 30 days prior to your birthday to 30 after your birthday is the time when you can be tested. This is random?

I have never tested any type of drug, recreational or otherwise, and I have no anticipation of ever doing so. I also detest the fact that our youth and not only our youth, but also grandparents alike, are destroying themselves daily by the use of drugs. I honestly feel that drugs and drugs alone will be the downfall of this wonderful country of ours. I also feel that neither the punishment nor the fear of punishment is strong enough to deter the use of drugs.

Look at the so-called idols of our youth today. It seems as though half of them are on drugs or are on a path of self -destruction.

Ok, so I will step down off of my soapbox on my feelings concerning drugs right after this. My question is this: If a person vacations or visits in a place where drug use is legal or accepted and participates in the using of these drugs and then returns to work in a week or so, what happens when this person is randomly tested and these drugs are still in that person's system, however the person is by no means impaired?

Impairment is the issue here. No firefighter who is impaired by any substance should be allowed to work. If a company officer has three firefighters under his command and one of them is impaired his manpower strength is not only reduced by one third, but that individual is now a liability to the company as a whole. It is for these reasons that I cannot ever see an impaired firefighter being allowed to report for duty.

Let's be honest here, as previously stated, the fire service is no different than any other occupation. I have the utmost respect for 95% of the firefighters I have ever met, but there is always that 5% that is questionable at best.

It has always been said that 95% of the local union's funds are spent to defend 5% of the membership. A truer statement has never been spoken.

While we are on the subject let's discuss fire chiefs who leave the fire service at a young age. In my career, I have met numerous chiefs who, at age 40 or so, are no longer fire chiefs. Why? Is it because of sickness? The city or town gets sick of them and no longer renews their contracts?

I have met firefighters who have such a desire to wear crossed bugles that I think they might sell their first born to become a 'chief'. Fire experience or not, how can an individual put him/herself in a position to be responsible for the safety of a number of firefighters at a fire scene when their experience is so limited?

I have always said that, other aspects aside, the most important qualification should be that a candidate for fire chief must have been in a burning building at least once in his or her life. That includes people whose only experience in the fire service has been as a dispatcher.

ᴣᴣᴣ

It has been said by a recent Fire Commissioner who today is no longer in command of the Boston Fire Department, "Where else can a person with a high school diploma get a job where they make $100,000."

Let's pick this quote apart. First, who is in charge of an organization and criticizes its members in such an unprofessional manner? If you headed a three hundred plus year old department, wouldn't you be proud of its heritage and its members and their accomplishments?

Secondly, why would you lie about the salary so that the public has an immediate envy in a time of economic distress? Maybe it wasn't a lie, but a matter of ignorance. After all he has only been the fire commissioner for a little over five years and I can understand how he hasn't had the time to investigate the salaries of his employees.

Thirdly, we address the issue of the high school diploma. I will give him the fact that a high school diploma is the minimum needed for appointment to the job. Many firefighters, fire lieutenants, fire captains, district chiefs and deputy chiefs have college degrees. Many have an associate's degree, many more a bachelor's degree. Even a few firefighters have a master's degree. Quite a few have had their degrees before they ever came on the job.

We have teachers, lawyers, instructors, nurses, EMTs and paramedics scattered throughout our 'high school diploma' workforce. We also employ firefighters who have worked as electricians, plumbers, carpenters, roofers, builders, iron workers, HVAC techs, auto body men, auto mechanics, and sheet metal workers, to name a few of the trades. Their knowledge can be invaluable at certain incidents.

For instance, at an incident involving an electrical situation the firefighter who has electrical knowledge will be called upon for his or her expertise. The same goes for a water hazard situation where both the plumber and the electrician are needed.

We respond to incidents of an odor in a building. At this type of incident, the HVAC tech is the go-to guy. At a particularly trying motor vehicle accident the auto body mechanic may have the expertise needed.

The list goes on and on, however there still will be the incident where no amount of knowledge, expertise, or training will be especially beneficial.

Training will be discussed in a later chapter. As you will find out then, the fire department trains on numerous aspects involving buildings, automobiles, the MBTA, the highway system, the waterfront, just to name a few. Even with all of this training there still will be incidents where the responding companies will be stumped by what they come across.

Take a recent trolley accident on the green line of the MBTA. The operator of the traveling trolley, which rear-ended a stopped trolley, lost her life in the accident. It was fairly quickly determined that the young woman was deceased. This incident then became a recovery rather than a rescue. The difference is that, in a rescue effort, speed is of the utmost importance. The victim must be medically stabilized and monitored throughout the rescue. The firefighters operating as rescue technicians are considering the speed of the extrication as well as the safety of the patient and themselves.

No matter how aware of safety, involvement in a rescue extrication presents hazards, which are uncommon to other situations. Injuries may occur just because of the hazardous nature of the entrapment or the surroundings of the situation.

The trolley accident involved an extrication that continued for several hours into the night. The steel front end of the trolley presented some problems never encountered prior to this accident.

While we train frequently with the MBTA, this accident presented some unique problems never before encountered. At the same time that one team was performing the extrication other teams were attending to the dozens of injured passengers aboard both trolleys.

This is one, and only one, of recent tragedies that firefighters respond to on a daily basis.

In addition to these firefighters and fire officers with technical knowledge and experience, we also have others who spend their free time studying and learning. Some may be studying for promotional examinations while some may be attending Emergency Medical Technician training or the Paramedic training that some are motivated to attain. Others may be attending higher education courses with a degree in the future.

We have Deputy Chiefs who have been promoted four times, District Chiefs who have been promoted three times, Fire Captains who have been promoted twice and Fire Lieutenants who have been promoted.

Some of our most brilliant members have remained in the ranks as firefighters because of many reasons. Some of those reasons are the inability to comprehend material from books or, perhaps, an inability to test well under the pressure of a timed examination involving thirty or more pages of reading, comprehension and decision-making. Poor reading skills might cause many to struggle. We have others who don't feel comfortable with the responsibility of having the lives and safety of their peers in their hands.

Yet, some of these members are our most capable, most knowledgeable firefighters in the field. Many of the individuals whom I have the most respect for on the job have been the firefighters 'on the back step'. This shows how firefighters are resistant to change. We have not ridden on the back step since the early 70s, yet we still refer to the back step firefighter.

I always remind newly promoted lieutenants how the actions of their subordinates, the firefighters under their command are the key forces in making your company look good at an incident. One of the most important things, not to be overlooked, is to communicate back to your firefighters the comments of a ranking officer when you receive praise for a job well done when it is bestowed upon you.

We have people on our job who have invented tools, written books, taught in college classrooms and taught our new recruits the skills that they need for a successful career.

I have always been impressed by the fact that it is easier to become a lawyer than it is to be promoted to fire lieutenant.

To become a lawyer, it takes attendance at a law school and then you have to pass the bar exam.

To become a fire lieutenant you have to study fourteen books for up to two years. It is not enough to pass the exam for fire lieutenant, but you must place high enough to be within the number of people promoted in a two-year period.

For fire lieutenant that number may be as high as 40, for fire captain as high as 20 and for district chief as high as 8. For deputy chief, many lists go by with no promotions or maybe one or two. Imagine how difficult it must be to be motivated enough to study for up to two years when you know that there may be no chance for promotion if you pass the examination.

With all of these facts I think that one can draw a conclusion that the fire commissioner does not hold his members in very high esteem. Too bad, his loss!

Myth Number Eight

Firefighters make a ton of money.

Up until the turn of the century firefighters might have made a lot of money, but they didn't make it on their fire department pay check.

Just about every firefighter I have ever met worked a 'side job'. Everybody had a part time job. Today this have changed somewhat. A firefighter's part time job today is being Mister Mom. The times have changed and they have changed for firefighters as well.

The population in general is marrying later. Women have had the opportunity to achieve a career for themselves. Therefore it is much more beneficial for the wives to work and the fathers to stay home and spend more quality time with their children.

Women appreciate being appreciated. Husbands know that the wives are probably more adept at earning a better salary than the husbands can earn at a part time job.

While I must admit that the fire department is paying firefighters a much better pay check than they did when I started ($137), it is still not enough to raise a family of two adults and the two and a half children that the model family is said to have.

So yes, firefighters may make a ton of money, but it is only through working a second job or through a second worker in the family that they are doing so.

Myth Number Nine

Firefighters sleep on the job.

While it is no secret that firehouses have bunkrooms and the omnipresent bunks, firefighters don't have a 'bed time' and they almost never have the uninterrupted night's sleep that other occupations enjoy when they go to bed at night.

I like to refer to it as 'resting between alarms'. While I may have spent a few hours every night tour lying in my bed, I very rarely slept as soundly as I did at home.

Firefighters work an average of 42 hours a week over an eight week cycle. Most employees of 'normal' jobs work either 40 or 37 ½ hours per week, every week.

Your mind is never at ease. You hear everything that is going on, every alarm whether your company responds or not, the department radio chattering all night, and of course the many runs to which you are summoned throughout the night as well as during the day.

Firefighters who work at busy companies may never get to put their ass in the bed at all. So while firefighters are bashed by political leaders and occasionally the public, we do get the opportunity to rest for a while when we are not dashing out the door to serve the public which pays our salary.

When we are not responding to a call for help whether it be a fire, medical assistance, or some of the myriad of other service calls that we do for the general public, don't deny us time to eat or time to get off of our feet for a short while.

This bears repeating; ours is the only job without a designated lunch or dinner hour.

Myth Number Ten

It's raining there will be no fires tonight.

I can't tell you how many times I have heard this one.

As a matter of fact my own father used to say this to me when I would be going in for a night tour. Oh yeah, he only said it to get my ass since he knew how much it pissed me off. I used to reply that some of the greatest fires that I have ever had were on nights of rain, sleet, and/or snow. He knew that his statement aggravated me so he used it all the more often.

One fact about rainy weather that exacerbates fire conditions is that misty, heavy wet air tends to hold down the smoke so that it doesn't rise into the atmosphere.

I have seen days and nights when the damp atmosphere keeps the smoke so low that when you come down the street you can't even tell which building is on fire.

I remember years ago Paul Bateman on Ladder 7 was telling me when I relieved him in the morning about a fire during the night tour when the smoke was so bad that when he threw the aerial to the house on fire he accidentally knocked the chimney over because of the terrible smoke condition.

I said, "Hey Paul, shit happens. It's just great that no one got hurt by the falling bricks."

His reply to me was, "No, you don't understand. I knocked the chimney down on the house next door."

I always said that this great job of ours would be even better if we could just do something about the smoke.

ﾉﾉﾉﾍ

Firefighters have always taken the opportunity to admire the ladies, both young and older, as they pass by firehouses. No woman passes without feeling the eyeballs of the members checking them out.

One of the most famous firehouses in the city in these terms is Engine 33 and Ladder 15 at 941 Boylston Street in the Back Bay. This firehouse sits right on the sidewalk and you can smell the perfumes and the shampoos as the travelers pass by. There is always something for everyone and the after shave might be the turn-on for some.

Thousands of times annually these companies respond to alarms and have continually been either the busiest or next-to-busiest firehouse in the city.

Visitors from across the state and across the country have stopped here. Visitors from foreign lands have also graced the doors of this firehouse. It seems everyone wants to go home with a t-shirt from the Back Bay firehouse which is home to Engine 33 and Ladder 15. "Keep back 300 feet" graces the back side of the shirt which is usually the flat side. The front may be the hilly side depending upon who will be wearing the pink, grey or blue t-shirt.

This firehouse sits in the shadow of the Prudential Tower which is part of the Prudential Center. It is a fifty-two story high-rise office tower. Originally the highest building in the city when it was built in the 60s, it has given away that title to the John Hancock tower. The Hancock tower, built in the 70s, is 60 stories.

The behemoth rising across the street from Engine 33's firehouse is surrounded by high-rise residential buildings, hotels, and parking garages. The mezzanine level is home to many specialty shops and restaurants.

The firehouse on Boylston Street was built in 1884 and is a beautiful architectural example of Boston's unique buildings. The firehouse floor had to be lowered on the ladder truck's side so that the rear mount aerial ladders of today could fit into the arched doorways.

Another fact of city life is that the trolleys of the Boylston Street subway tunnel run directly under the street in front of the firehouse and one can feel the rumble hundreds of times daily as they pass by beneath the street.

The Back Bay is home to hundreds of beautiful buildings built on filled in land. Originally part of the Charles River, this area was made usable by fill being moved into the area from the Fort Hill Square area in Downtown Boston. This is the only section of the city where the streets are all laid out in an east to west and north to south pattern. The main streets running east to west are Boylston, Newbury, Marlborough and Beacon Streets and Commonwealth Avenue with its stately mall running down the center of the avenue.

Another unique fact is that the cross streets are all in alphabetical order starting at the east with Arlington Street, followed by Berkeley, Clarendon, Dartmouth, Exeter, Fairfield, Gloucester, and Hereford Streets.

In between the east to west streets are a series of Public Alleys all running one block long and all numbered consecutively. These public alleys are usually the areas where garages are situated and the not-so-pleasant area where the rubbish is collected weekly.

Lois is a young lady who conducts business nightly on Hereford Street. For a fee one may rent her for a few minutes of warmth and 'love'. She may occupy the alley behind the firehouse numerous times each night, sometimes in a car and sometimes in a van. She has even been spotted entertaining clients in the open air.

The Back Bay is a haven for men of any age to show their dates a unique and interesting night out. There are too many to count restaurants lining Boylston and Newbury Streets. The outdoor café seating fills up fast and is in demand from April through October. High end shops line Newbury St. selling everything from footwear to lingerie to sweets.

One of the best businesses, in my opinion, is the parking business where everyone must pay a ransom to claim their car at the end of an expensive night out on the town.

Peter and Jamie arrived in the Back Bay one evening from a western suburb of Boston. It was Jamie's birthday and Peter was holding nothing back from showing Jamie the time of her life. First they circled the area looking for a parking spot. When Peter realized that this search would be futile he stopped at a valet spot and turned the keys to his Lexus over to a cowboy with a red jacket. Once Peter escorted Jamie from the car, his Lexus was whisked off to NeverNeverland.

After a $150 dinner at the Capitol Grille Peter and Jamie took in a movie at a theatre in Copley Place. After the movie and an espresso at an Italian café along with pastries for a night cap, they returned to the valet to claim the Lexus.

Twenty minutes later, as Peter opened the door so the lovely Jamie could slide her long shapely legs into the leather seat giving the red jacketed valet a glimpse of pink undies as her short skirt slid even higher than planned.

As the Lexus sped up Newbury St. headed for the west bound entrance to the Massachusetts Turnpike, Peter ran a short yellow light which turned red before they were even into the intersection. Almost immediately a van heading south broadsided the Lexus on Jamie's side.

The 911 call center immediately started receiving calls reporting a very bad accident at Massachusetts Avenue and Newbury St. with people trapped inside the car and the van.

The Boston Fire Department Fire Alarm Office received box 1584 at Mass and Commonwealth Avenues. The tones at Engine 33 were activated and the house lights came on as the Fire Alarm Office announced, "Engine 33, Ladder 15, Car 4, respond to Box 1584, Commonwealth and Massachusetts Aves."

The member on patrol at 941 Boylston St. hit the house alarm and announced the same message which came over the radio. The firefighters on the second floor all headed for the poles as the members who had been sitting on the bench outside came in to don their bunker gear and head out to Mass. and Comm.

As the chauffeurs turned over the diesel engines on the Pierce pumper and ladder truck, the officers sounded the sirens as the companies rolled slowly over the threshold and turned right onto Boylston Street. It was only one block over the turnpike bridge to Mass. Ave. and then two blocks north to Commonwealth Avenue, but the mess of automobile wreckage at Newbury Street completely blocked Mass Ave. It was quickly determined that this accident was the reason the box had been pulled.

The members of the Engine pulled a 1 ¾" line off the rig and advanced it to the impact point while the truckies from Ladder 15 began to remove the Amkus tool from the truck. The Captain of Ladder 15 called on the radio reporting an auto accident with entrapment and requested the services of Rescue One.

Fire Alarm repeated the message and advised Ladder 15 that Rescue One was already responding after receiving numerous calls for the accident.

Inside the van were three guys and a girl and various musical instruments. The driver and passenger were pretty messed up and appeared to be trapped inside the van. An investigation of the Lexus, or what was left of the Lexus revealed two patients, one of which was trapped. The blonde girl in the passenger seat was grossly trapped and appeared severely injured.

As the officer of Engine 33 reported to Fire Alarm on the number of entrapments and patients the members of Ladder had the 'Jaws' running and were beginning to cut the metal which was mangled and entrapped the woman in the Lexus.

One member of Engine 33 stood by with the hose line and the others began using hand tools to attempt extrication of the passengers in the van.

Soon the sirens of the rescue were heard coming down Beacon St. to Mass. Ave. It had only been about four minutes and the firefighters of Engine 33 and Ladder 15 were glad that another Amkus tool was on the scene to assist in the extrication.

Rescue One members used the jaws and the cutters at the same time to work on both vehicles. The two patients in the front of the van were easily removed. The two riding in the rear were bounced around with the musical instruments. None of the four seemed too badly injured

Boston EMS arrived with a supervisor, two BLS units and an ALS unit. The EMTs started to treat the occupants of the van while the medics prepared their equipment to treat the young lady in the Lexus. The driver of the car was able to free himself in spite of the door being wedged closed.

The woman was covered with a blanket as the windshield was removed and the two tools worked side by side to extricate her. In a short time the doors were removed and the backboard was slid under the blonde's derriere. The members of Rescue 1 slid her body around until she was stable on the board. They removed her from the passenger area and placed the backboard on the ground so that the medics could start treating her injuries. Her right thigh was the recipient of quite a large laceration as well as her head. Blood was profusely flowing, but the injuries were not as severe as originally thought.

During the confusion the district chief of District Four arrived and assumed command. He did little to interfere with the operation since he knew that these patients were in the hands of some of the most qualified and capable members of the department. He knew that as soon as the patients were extricated the paramedics and EMTs of Boston EMS would show their professionalism in caring for the injuries.

In short time everyone was out of the vehicles and the scene was secured for the Boston Police to conduct their investigation of the accident.

The district chief informed the lieutenant of Rescue One that they could run along as soon as their equipment was made up. He also dismissed the engine and the ladder truck and notified Fire Alarm that the scene was being cleared with a code 322 and a 413. The 413 covers the hazardous materials incident that was generated because of the need for hazardous liquids being spilled onto the street.

Last year these fire companies did almost 4000 incident responses. That does not include the drills, the inspections or the driver trainings. Since they are some of the busiest companies in the city, every time they roll on an incident the possibility of another response for them having to be covered by another fire house is a distinct reality.

CHAPTER 3

Fire Buffs, Sparks, Fire Fans

You may have heard of characters who chase fires and perhaps take photos of fires. They are known by different names depending upon where in the country you find them.

In the northeast these characters are known as 'sparks' or 'sparkies'. Throughout many areas they are 'buffs' and to some they are just plain 'whackos'. Most of these individuals do not chase fires and fire engines just see a building burn. Their main interest is in watching the firefighting operation. They enjoy arriving early on in the beginning stages so that they witness, or perhaps, 'study' the firefighting operations.

Many buffs take photos of the fire, the firefighting operations or the firefighters themselves. Two of the most famous fire photographers that I know are Bill Noonan from Boston and Steve Spak from New York City. These two guys have made a career out of their hobby of taking photos of the firefighters. Both have published books which are basically firefighting journals containing hundreds of photos of both men and women firefighters. These firefighters are the personnel of both big-city and rural, small town America fire departments.

Firefighters in action, making rescues, or just doing their jobs are the focus of fire photographers. Group photos of the various fire companies are the interest of Bill Noonan. Steve Spak loves the action photos from the FDNY.

Two more individuals that I have known for forty years are Stanley Forman and George Rizer. These two have been shooting photos for the news service for years. George, now retired, worked for the Boston Globe. Stan used to work for the Boston Herald and now is a freelancer who has changed his specialty over the years from still photos to videography.

Stanley Forman has also been the proud recipient of two Pulitzer Prizes. One was for his set of action photos taken in 1975 depicting the tragic collapse of a balcony fire escape in the Back Bay section of Boston. At this fire a young woman was killed in a five story fall and her toddler relative survived while landing on the adult victim. This was a horrific tragedy captured by a man who has spent his entire life photographing news stories.

Stanley's other Pulitzer involved a victim of racial strife who was beset upon by an attacker armed with an American flag.

♪♪♪♪

Unfortunately, it is true that not all of the people who chase fires are doing it for a hobby or to preserve history in the photos that are taken. Some of these people are disturbed and may actually have had a role in the start of the fire. Thankfully the number of such incidents is few and the perpetrators are the subject of fire investigation units nationwide.

Fire photographers fall into many categories. I enjoy photographing firehouses, some take photos of fire apparatus, some take action shots. Most photographers collect their photos, some sell them. Many use their photos as a source of income by publishing books, printing calendars or just plain trying to make a buck by selling their work to Associated Press or the local news outlet.

I have been a spark since I was about 14. My uncle from Rhode Island was involved with the Warwick, R I fire department many, many years ago. I visited there and he always had the fire radio on. He took me along with him to many incidents when I was much younger.

I remember one particular fire in the Conimicut section of Warwick that we went to one night. The fire was in a bungalow with gasoline shingles. The house was pretty much gutted and I thought that it was a terrible situation. I actually had nightmares about this fire for months after.

Another extremely large fire we took in was the roller rink not too far in from Cranston. I was really interested in this whole fire department thing.

When I was a young teenager I saved enough money to purchase a Realistic low band fire radio from Radio Shack. The radio was a tunable model so you were able to hear many fire departments. Boston Fire was 33.76 MHz on the dial and if you played a little with the dial you could pick up Cambridge, Somerville, Newton and Brookline along with Boston all at the same time.

Nobody in my family ever drove and so when I turned 16 and became a licensed driver I was actually able to get in my car and go to fires. I was in heaven. I met fellow sparks. I learned so much about the fire department operations.

I became friendly with a fellow named Mike Iervolino. Mike was originally from Brockton, MA. He married a girl from South Boston and was living in South Boston when I met him in 1963. Mike was a member of the Boston Fire Department Auxiliary. The company was called CD-10 (as in Civil Defense). He told me to stop by the firehouse some Saturday night.

I found Engine 16's former firehouse in Mattapan and visited quite frequently. I had a strong desire to become a member of this outfit, but I could not join until I reached my 18th birthday. You can bet I was waiting at the door on the night I turned 18.

I became a member of CD-10 in 1964 and continued to volunteer here until October, 1969. I was a member of the duty crew on Saturday nights. I later picked up an occasional Sunday night. When I was 'promoted' to lieutenant I took over Monday nights, group 1.

This was the time of my life. I was single, working a great day time job with the U S Post Office and spent what seemed like half of my life at 2 Temple St. I met the greatest bunch of guys in my five years here. Most continued on to become firefighters in Boston.

The firefighters union wasn't exactly happy about us doing their jobs for free. Today with the much stronger unions Engine Company CD-10 would never work. Work was something we did well. We were in service most afternoons, evenings and nights.

Whenever there was a major fire in Boston or a second alarm fire in the surrounding communities, there were always at least four or five maniacs on the road heading to 2 Temple St. to man Engine Company CD-10.

The bulk of our responses were to the cities of Chelsea, Brookline, Milton, Revere and Winthrop. Oftentimes we covered at a vacant firehouse, but very often responded to the fire. What a great training tool. We all had our own gear which we bought ourselves.

There were so many of us that went on to be firefighters and fire officers in the Boston Fire Department.

Jim Ochs became a firefighter on Ladder 23 and then a lieutenant on Ladder 7 and 23. Don Taber was a firefighter and lieutenant on Engine 52, I became a lieutenant on Engine 10, Rescue 1 and then the captain of Engine 10. Bob 'Herbie' Winston was a firefighter on Ladder 29 and later became a District Chief. Paul Finn was a firefighter on Ladder 20 and Engine 21 and then a lieutenant on Engine 33 and Engine 8.

We had firefighter Bob Cassell on Engine 42 and 21, Charlie Seaboyer on Engine 18, the infamous Kenny Rogers who worked on Engine 24 for many years before becoming a District Chief's aide to a couple of chiefs, Vin Bolger and Jim Freeman.

Third District I. A. F. F. Vice President Mike Mullane, a member of Engine 21, Bob Lindsay of Ladder 23, Steve Nawoichik of Engine 21, Herb Pearlstein was a member of Ladder 8 and Engine 55.

Tom Hurley became a federal firefighter with the U S Navy in Charlestown and in New York City. He later was a firefighter in Nashua, NH. Charlie Hanlon was a fire alarm operator in the BFD. Chuck Bazylinski was a member of Somerville Engine 7 forever, I think. Phil 'Killer' Kane was a firefighter in Abington, MA.

Jack Blackmore was an auxiliary firefighter in Somerville for many years. Bill Olson was a call firefighter in Hanover, MA and later became a chief in his home village in Florida.

You will notice that there was no one assigned to quiet companies out of this group. I feel it necessary to tell you about this great group of characters. I met them all here and we all went on to the greatest career in the world.

Spark is the term used around this part of the country to describe an individual who likes to chase fires, photograph fires and firefighters and has an all-around interest in the fire service. There have been many famous sparks in this area. The most famous were Boston Pops conductor Arthur Fiedler, Ben Ellis who owned Ellis Fire Appliance Company, the late mayor of New York City Fiorello LaGuardia and Dave Mugar, a philanthropist whose generosity helps guarantee a 4th of July spectacular every year in Boston.

CHAPTER **4**

Arson in Boston

In the 1970s there was an arson plague along Dudley Street in Roxbury. Every night between 4pm and 8pm some building along Dudley St. would burn. Some of these fires were accidental, but the vast majority of them were incendiary in nature.

The perpetrator would set the fires in the first floor public hallway. From there the fire would race up the stairs to the top floor. Along its path, if any door happened to be open, the fire would enter the apartment and make its new home inside. Many of these apartment buildings were vacant so the doors may have been left open or else they may have been removed completely.

Usually, in occupied buildings the doors would be closed and the fire went up until it had nowhere else to go. Some of these tenants on the top floor would open their apartment doors and were met with violent, searing heat followed by the raging fire.

Many occupants were killed by the wanton acts of a deranged person. These buildings had no storage space so the front halls became a storage area by the residents for baby carriages, bicycles, spare tires, even mattresses. This problem became the starting point for an arsonist's rage. Occasionally the junk collected here became a detriment to easy escape from the upper floors and an obstruction to the entry of firefighters.

One must realize that when a fire starts in an enclosed area the heat, smoke and toxic gases rise through convection currents which carry these elements of combustion to the roof area where they have no place further to travel. Once the smoke, heat and gases are trapped in their vertical ascent, they spread out laterally until the walls contain them.

The products of combustion now begin their descent back down to the opening, if any, on the first floor. At this point, if the front door is closed, anyone making entry may be subject to a blast of heat and, possibly, fire seeking fresh air for its continued combustion. If the area is devoid of any openings, the oxygen required for sustained combustion is being consumed rapidly. The opening of any door or window satisfies the fire's craving for more oxygen with sometimes explosive results.

This is commonly known as backdraft. The word backdraft is relatively new in the fire service. In the 1950s, 60s and 70s this phenomenon was usually referred to as a hot air explosion.

Arson in the Seventies

The characters involved in the following arsons were despicable.

It happened over and over in the seventies along Symphony Rd. in the Fenway area. Arson!

These fires were not isolated to Symphony Road, but were also happening on Gainsborough St., Westland Avenue and Hemenway St. These fires usually struck in the early morning hours, but oftentimes even earlier, in the pre-midnight hours.

Hundreds of people burned out of their homes, some even *killed* in the mysterious fires, dozens of injuries to firefighters and civilians alike. Millions of dollars in destroyed property and possessions.

Some dubious real estate businessmen and malicious landlords were the culprits. It would take many months and even years to prove the suspicions of the residents and the fire department alike.

❧❧❧

According to Jim Botticelli, creator of the Facebook page, *Dirty Old Boston*, "The neighborhood is burning nightly and there's nothing you can do but wait in fear."

"That is exactly what happened during the 1970s as Boston residents were under siege. Real estate businessmen were making money by burning apartment buildings to the ground leaving the poor, the elderly, and minority tenants homeless and several dead."

"The tenants' cries for arson investigation were dismissed. Arson was hard to prosecute and arson for profit was business as usual across the nation."

"A brave group of community activists refused to be silent victims. Their hard work revealed a shocking pattern to the fires and it was enough to convince the state to prosecute and eventually convict 32 men in a conspiracy bigger than anyone suspected."

"During the mid-1970s nearly every building on the one block long Symphony Road burned in just a four year period."

"Located in the shadows of Symphony Hall in the Fenway neighborhood, the street was the scene of a conspiracy that took the lives of local tenants including a four year old boy."

"And, as with so many crimes, money was the motive. At the time arson was hard to convict and rarely prosecuted, making it a lucrative and low risk crime."

"Tenants in the Fenway had worked hard to build their neighborhood into their homes. It wasn't just people living in close proximity, it was a community."

"When arson for profit targeted Symphony Road, the tenants refused to sit by and become victims of the violence threatening their homes and their lives. Despite being told repeatedly that they themselves were the problem and the source of the fires, the tenants were able to prove they were, in fact, victims of a large arson conspiracy."

Botticelli has a documentary to be soon released called Burning Greed.

Arson in the Eighties

The characters committing these arsons had warped minds. Their intent was supposedly for the restoration of fire companies and firefighting positions, but the destruction of property was in the millions of dollars. The number of injuries to firefighters was staggering.

After the fire company closings and the layoff of hundreds of firefighters in 1981 and 1982 a group was secretly formed to attempt to force the City of Boston and other cities and towns to rehire their firefighters.

This arson case and the subsequent convictions of the arsonists was the largest of its kind since the Symphony Road arson convictions in the mid-70s.

Federal officials charged that the group which was made up mostly of police officers, firefighters, security guards and firefighter wannabes set the fires in 1981 and 1982 that entitled Boston as "The arson capital of the world".

According to then, United States Attorney William F. Weld, "The fires were set to scare the public into supporting more positions for police and fire departments after property tax reductions had reduced their ranks by layoffs and hiring freezes."

Federal agents arrested six people in three states charging them with arson. A seventh person turned himself in to authorities in Boston. According to records two of the defendants were armed when arrested.

The five arrested in the Boston area pleaded not guilty at their hearing. More charges and arrests were expected.

U S Attorney Weld said that the 83 count Federal indictment announced was believed to be "the largest single arson case in history, state or federal, in terms of the number of fires involved."

The indictment alleges that beginning sometime after July 1981, as the effect of a state wide tax cutting measure referred to as Proposition 2 ½ forced layoffs on hundreds of police officers and firefighters in Massachusetts, the members of the group set 163 fires in Boston and nine surrounding cities and towns. The outlying fires were set to divert investigators away from Boston, the indictment said.

It also said that the defendants who worked for a security company burned a client's building to distract attention from themselves.

The buildings burned included houses, churches, factories, restaurants, a Marine Corps barracks and the Massachusetts Firefighting Academy. These fires accounted for 281 firefighters suffering injuries, many of which were career ending injuries for some.

The fires listed in the indictment grew in frequency and number over the months. They stirred deep public apprehension here, generated local and national news accounts, and two years ago resulted in the Federal investigation that produced the indictments.

District Attorneys of five counties, the Federal Bureau of Investigation and the Federal Bureau of Alcohol, Tobacco, and Firearms were all involved in the indictments. One district attorney called the case "the most frightening and bizarre criminal conspiracy I have ever seen."

Who's Burning Boston?

Mr. Higgins held up copies of Boston magazines of the period that he said published cover articles asking the question " Who's burning Boston?"

"We're here today because we think these charges are a step toward answering that question," Mr. Higgins said.

"The indictments allege perjury, obstruction of justice, threatening of witnesses and destruction of evidence, as well as conspiracy. Affidavits presented at a Federal bail hearing this afternoon further allege that one of the defendants threatened to kill the supervisor in the Bureau of Alcohol, Tobacco and Firearms who led the investigation."

Other defendants, the affidavits allege, urged a Boston police officer who had already pleaded guilty in the case to flee to Canada before sentencing. He was subsequently sentenced to state and Federal prison terms and is expected to be a witness in the Federal trials.

Clubs of 'Fire Buffs'

At the hearing for the men arrested in the Boston area, a Federal magistrate ordered Donald Stackpole, Gregg M. Bemis and Wayne S. Sanden held without bail, and set bail for Ray J. Norton, Jr. and Joseph M. Gorman at $50,000 and $25,000, respectively.

U. S. Attorney Weld said the group had had its genesis in a little-known but organized world of people fascinated by fires. "My understanding is that there are certain clubs in Boston where fire buffs are known to hang out," he said.

Boston has had three well known clubs for fire buffs, The Tapper Club, The Box 52 Association and the Boston Sparks Association.

The clubs are legitimate organizations of people drawn to fires and firefighting, Mr. Weld said, and one of them, The Boston Sparks Association, was burned by the defendants after it refused to admit Mr. Stackpole and Mr. Bemis as members.

Stackpole, 28 years old, of Scituate, a partner in a South Boston security company, is charged with conspiracy, arson and obstruction of justice.

Bemis, 23, of South Boston, a sergeant in the Boston Housing Authority Police Department, is charged with those crimes as well as with mailing threatening communications.

Sanden, 28, of the Roslindale section of Boston, a lieutenant in the Housing Authority Police, is charged with conspiracy, arson and obstruction of justice.

Mr. Norton, 44, of West Roxbury, a Boston firefighter, is charged with conspiracy, perjury, and aiding and abetting arson.

Mr. Gorman, 27, of Quincy, a rigger for the General Dynamics plant in Quincy, is charged with conspiracy, and aiding and abetting arson.

Other Defendants:

Christopher R. Damon, 27, who was arrested in Hamilton, Ohio, and is an employee of a company named Industrial Health, is charged with conspiracy, and aiding and abetting arson.

Leonard A. Kendall Jr., 22, of Acton, who was arrested in Valdosta, Ga., where he is a United States Air Force enlisted man serving as a fireman, is charged with conspiracy, arson and perjury.

One of these fires was set in the offices of the Gay Community News on Bromfield Street in Downtown Boston. This fire went to 7 alarms and destroyed everything in the entire building. While the building was gutted, the structure itself was saved and has been completely rebuilt.

During the week of November 14th, 1982, once again the familiar flames flickered in the night sky over Boston. Again there were the shouted commands, the blur of moving figures playing out the hoses, the crackle of the dispatchers' voices on the radio, the ascending roar of the fire.

The Gerrity Lumberyard in Hyde Park burned on Nov. 21, 1982, in the middle of a series of fires that staggered the city's resources and imagination.

On Tuesday, on the 12th floor of the post office building in downtown Boston, that fire burned again on television as a Federal jury watched a videotape made by a television camera operator that night.

The camera shifted to the side, and there, seated or leaning against a pile of lumber, watching, was a group of men who were seen at many of the fires that broke out in 1982 and 1983. As the camera recorded it, one of the men grinned broadly, and waved a gun in the air. Trial for Arson

He was Robert Groblewski, a Boston police officer now in Federal prison after pleading guilty to conspiracy and other arson charges stemming from the fires.

To his right, as the camera stayed on the group, was Donald F. Stackpole, a partner in a private security company. It is Mr. Stackpole who is on trial here now, on multiple conspiracy and arson charges to which he has pleaded not guilty.

To Mr. Stackpole's right were Joseph M. Gorman, a rigger at the General Dynamics plant in Quincy, and Ray J. Norton, Jr., a Boston firefighter. Mr. Gorman, since then, has also pleaded guilty to arson charges and is serving five years in prison. Mr. Norton, who used to drive to work at the fire department in a car with the license plate "ARSON," has pleaded not guilty to Federal arson charges and is awaiting trial.

And in the middle of this strange group, in this strange story of public policy, fires, and people drawn by fire, was Gregg M. Bemis, 24 years old, who took the witness stand to testify against Mr. Stackpole as the trial got under way.

It was Mr. Bemis, by his own confession, who had set the lumberyard fire. He called himself "Mr. Flare," and he confessed to setting many of the 264 fires that the Federal authorities say were set by this group. They destroyed more than $30 million in property, injured more than 360 people, and all together they constitute the largest arson case in the history of the United States, the United States Attorney, William F. Weld, has said.

The group set the fires, a Federal grand jury charged, because a property tax referendum had forced the layoffs of hundreds of fire-fighters and police officers in Massachusetts, threatening the jobs of men like Mr. Norton and Mr. Groblewski, and threatening the prospects of others who wanted to be firefighters.

Mr. Gorman had applied to be a state trooper and "Groblewski, Sanden and Bemis had all taken the exam to be firefighters and were on the list eligible to be hired," said Mark E. Robinson, the Assistant United States Attorney who is prosecuting the case. Wayne S. Sanden, who has also pleaded guilty to conspiracy and arson charges, was a lieutenant with the Boston Housing Authority Police Department, where Mr. Bemis was a sergeant. While they waited to be hired as firefighters, the authorities say, they spent their spare time setting fires.

The rationale for these fires, the grand jury charged, was to alarm the public into restoring funds for firefighting and police jobs.

Confusing Hobby with Arson

If the public was stunned by the notion that public servants would burn down buildings to drum up support for jobs, the smaller but ardent national culture of fire hobbyists was dismayed at the idea of being confused in the public's mind with an arson ring.

At the fires that Mr. Bemis set in the middle of the night, and then turned up to watch, there were often dozens of other citizens, some with cameras and some with special gold-plated badges that the City of Boston authorized for members of the three fire clubs here, who turned up for the occasions of their favorite hobby: fires.

In Chicago, said Dennis Williams, a former president of the International Fire Buffs Association, the hobbyists are called "Fire Fans," in New York, "Fire Buffs" and in Boston, "Sparks."

It is a strong tradition here. Arthur Fiedler, the late conductor of the Boston Pops, was a famous spark. Richard Bangs, executive secretary of the Boston Sparks' Association, remembers the night that a former Fire Commissioner gave Mr. Fiedler and the impresario Ed Sullivan a ride to the waterfront, where they watched a building blaze against the darkness of Boston Harbor.

Commemorating 1872 Fire

The oldest fire-buffs club in the country, Box 52, is headquartered here, founded in 1912 by a group whose successors still hold an annual dinner, as they did last Friday, to commemorate the Great Boston Fire of 1872.

Box 52 situated at the corner of Summer and Lincoln Streets was the alarm box pulled for the Great Boston Fire.

The last convention of the International Fire Buffs Association, with 80 chapters around the country, was held here in Boston in July, 1984 the month that the Federal indictments were released.

But the Boston Sparks Association, and its clubs, have a code "of gentlemanly conduct" and a screening process to keep out people who act irresponsibly.

George Paul, who was the Fire Commissioner here until 1984, said he had been aware of Mr. Stackpole for 12 or 14 years. He was conspicuous, Mr. Paul said, because he would arrive at a fire dressed in a kind of uniform, driving a station wagon like a fire company wagon, "with flashing orange or green lights."

Waiting for Fires

Mr. Robinson, the prosecutor, told the trial jury that Mr. Stackpole, Mr. Bemis and the rest of the group came to know each other in a parking lot where sparks used to gather at night across from the fire department, listening to their scanners, waiting for a fire.

For many sparks, fires have been a lifelong attraction, and as Albert Bielitz, Mr. Bemis's attorney, discovered the night before Mr. Bemis was sentenced to 30 years in Federal prison, Mr. Bemis's mother was a spark.

She took her child to fires. "That continued until he was 17 years old, at which time she died," Mr. Bielitz said. After the boy's first visit to his mother's grave, Mr. Bielitz said, he set his first fire in a nearby field. For the next four years, until Mr. Bemis met other members of the group at 21, Mr. Bielitz said, he set a fire after each visit to his mother's grave.

One of the more notable fires that Mr. Bemis helped to set, as he said on the witness stand this week, was the one that burned down the clubhouse of the Boston Sparks Association, whose membership had grown suspicious of the group.

But it was not until Mr. Bemis was in jail, and unable to set any more fires, Mr. Bielitz said, that his client realized, fully, finally, that his mother was dead. It was then that Mr. Bemis broke down, Mr. Bielitz said, and told this story, of fire and love.

CHAPTER **5**

The Boston Fire Department Work Schedule

The BFD work schedule has always been an interesting one. For the 48 hour week there were seven groups or shifts as some fire departments call them. Two of these groups worked at a time. Groups 2 and 3 may work in the day with group 6 and 7 working at night. This rotation was followed the next day with groups 3 and 4 working in the day and group 7 and 1 working at night. Two day tours were followed by 24 hours off and then two night tours, followed by three days off. This rotation continued until a Monday was encountered. When Monday arrived everything skipped ahead by a day and then followed until the next Monday. Simple wasn't it?

During the 46 hour work week there were eleven groups. Three groups worked at a time. If groups 2, 3, and 4 worked in the day, then groups 8, 9, and 10 worked at night. This was really a screwed up work schedule and I'm glad that it only lasted for 18 months.

At Engine 29 and Ladder 11 some brain surgeon decided that this schedule was an easy way to decide the watch rotation. The first numbered group would do the watch before midnight, 1800 until 2100 and then 2100 until midnight. The second numbered group would do the after midnight watches, midnight until 0400 and then 0400 until 0800. If the engine went out and an engine guy had the watch then a ladder guy would have to fill in until the engine came back.

This was almost as complicated as the work schedule, right?

There was only one problem with this watch rotation. I was alone on group 9 and there was only one ladder man on group 9. There were two firefighters on group 8 and group 10 on both companies. This meant that the group 9 guys had a watch every night and the same guy had the fill-in on our third night.

That schedule sucked, big time!

Finally with the start of the 42 hour work week at the end of June in 1971 there were four work groups. With previous schedules a firefighter in the field worked with different men on different days, but the 42 hour week saw four groups with each group becoming its own little 'fire department'. Firefighters worked with same firefighters, fire officers and chiefs each day and night that they worked. The rotation of the schedule was day, night, 24 off, day, night, 72 off.

Rivalry was fostered with group one being the number one group. It was rumored that group four does more. It seemed as though group three had all of the big fires, followed by group two. In reality, we all know that group four is the screwed up group. Ask anyone! Every fire department has its own group four.

I know that right now you are probably saying, "What a screwed up Fire Department". Well, it only took a short time to adjust to the schedule.

If you think that was easy to understand then I have to tell you that we also have a vacation schedule. Each member is assigned his/her vacation by being assigned to another group, your vacation group which has absolutely nothing to do with your work group.

The vacation schedule is figured out for years in advance. You may be assigned to two weeks in April and two weeks in October, but don't despair because when you have two weeks in July, you also will have the two weeks over Christmas. That happens about once every ten years.

Now, I realize that this sounds complicated, but you have the ability to swap with another member in your company. You also have the option of applying for a special vacation at the behest of the Deputy Fire Chief on your group on a first apply, first served option.

The official times of the group changes are 0800 and 1800. Since it is a job where one person relieves another, firefighters tend to relieve at times convenient to each other. Most arrive between 0700 and 0800 with a few exceptions arriving at 0759.

In the afternoon each firehouse seemed to develop its own relief time. Some downtown companies relieved by 1600 to beat the traffic and some relieved at 1755 to await the subsiding of the traffic. Some fire-fighters worked side jobs that did not allow them to get in before 1700; where others couldn't wait to get out of the house, away from the wife and kids, so they arrived any time after 1500.

Since we have unlimited tour swapping capabilities some firehouses started swapping tours so we could work 24 tours. The contract says we work 10s and 14s, but the majority of the on-duty crews are work-ing 24 hour tours by swapping. I personally worked these 24s for my last 14 or 15 years on the job.

We had one Commissioner who tried to limit the number of tours we could swap annually, but was beaten down in court by the infamous 'past practice' of allowing tour swapping without limitation.

The benefits of 24 hour tours are many with only a few bad features. I would have to say that the only negative aspect of the 24 hour tour is the holidays. If your group is scheduled to work a 24 hour tour on a holiday then you are a trapped audience and you will not get to spend any time on the holiday with your family. The only holidays that were important enough for me to make this an issue were Thanksgiving and Christmas.

The job is wonderful and has always treated me and my family well so this minor inconvenience has to be dealt with and it only happens on the average of once every four years.

When the 'Big Dig' started in 1997 the Fort Hill Square firehouse tried to convince the City that the opportunity to work 24 hour tours would benefit a lot of people. The traffic nightmares began and the members thought that one trip, once a day would be beneficial. It would also take some cars off of the road.

Our plan was shot down, but the devious minds of the firemen worked on a plan to make this work, with or without the approval of the BFD brass. It was determined that if the member working the night tour swapped on during the day tour and then the next night tour member swapped on during the next day tour all tours would be covered and everyone would be happy.

It was extremely easy and almost a no-brainer if you were in a category where all four groups were covered by the same people all of the time. Let me try to explain this better.

Officers on a company would all be doing the 24s. Chiefs in a district or a division would all be doing the 24s. Specialized outfits such as the air supply or the rehab unit would all be doing the 24s. The only ones who were left without a complete even number of members to do this would be the rank and file firefighters on a company.

If each company had three or four firefighters on every group then it would have worked, however when a member goes on vacation, gets injured, etc. there was a problem.

We also ran into a few members who would come to work in our firehouse for a short period such as an acting lieutenant or acting captain who needed to be contacted before he arrived so that we could tell him not to come in for his first day tour, but to come in the following day for 24.

In all of the years that we worked this schedule, I only saw one member come through our firehouse while an acting officer who refused to cooperate. Remember that Mike? Most people felt that it was, "When in Rome do as the Romans do."

The result of members seeing that this schedule really worked would go back to their own firehouses and talk it up.

One Deputy Chief refused to go along and upon his promotion the remaining deputies began working 24 hour tours the very next day.

One district chief refused to go along with the other three chiefs in his district, but would have to do 24s when he filled in at Division One in the deputy's car. His coworkers reminded him of this and he suddenly changed his mind about working 24s in his own district.

Peer pressure, nothing like it.

CHAPTER 6

My Appointment

When I was appointed in 1969, it was a period in the BFD when the day tours were busy and the night tours were even busier. I had high hopes of being appointed to a busy company. Ladder 4 was the object of my intentions.

In 1969 Ladder 4 was quartered alone at 198 Dudley Street in Roxbury. It was the lone firehouse in the city where only a ladder truck was quartered. One of the niceties was the fact that when you returned from a fire there was no hose to pack or hang in the hose tower to dry.

My goal was to get to Ladder 4, but that was not an easy task. I talked to the captain. John C. T. Hawe was the captain in the late sixties. A powerful, stern captain whose stature was small, but his firefighting abilities were enormous. Captain Hawe with his wavy gray hair, riding the running board of the ladder truck as it backed into quarters after a run is as vivid in memory as it was forty odd years ago.

My attempts to reach my goal did not stop there. One day a friend of mine introduced me to George Lee. Lee was a Fire Lieutenant assigned to the Fire Investigation Unit under the Fire Prevention Division. Since he worked out of Fire Headquarters and was a senior-most fire lieutenant, he familiar with the workings of the administrative offices. George Lee took me to see the Chief of Department, Joseph Kilduff.

Joe Kilduff was another stern fire officer who had a love for the job and, especially, for fighting fires in Roxbury. Lieutenant Lee introduced me as a young rookie, soon to be appointed firefighter, to the Chief. "Chief", he said, "This young fellow is coming on next week and he has a request."

"Yeah, what's that? I suppose he wants a quiet house out in the country", said Kilduff.

"No Sir", I replied. "Actually I was looking to go to Ladder 4."

"Ladder 4", he retorted. "What's wrong with Ladder 30?"

"Nothing, there is absolutely nothing wrong with Ladder 30. If I can't get to Ladder 4, then Ladder 30 would be wonderful", stammered the young boy whose knees were knocking as he stood before the top firefighter in the Boston Fire Department. Chief Kilduff scratched a note next to my name on the list before him. He wrote L4 or L30 and initialed his note, JEK.

As Chief Kilduff, Lieutenant Lee and I discussed the soon-to-be appointed recruit class, my expectations were put into high gear. The way that I figured, if the Chief of Department couldn't help, who could?

❧❧❧

Two nights later the General Order announcing the appointment of sixty Firefighters on Probation was published. I was at home and received a phone call from an old friend. My good friend and best man at my wedding was Tom Hurley. The call was from Tom's father Ed. Ed was a Fire Lieutenant on Engine 8. He was working and told me over the phone, "The orders are out".

I anxiously and nervously asked where I was going. "Is it Ladder 4 or Ladder 30?"

Ed hesitated and said softly, "I hate to tell you this, but you are going to Engine Company 29."

I almost dropped the phone. I couldn't be sure that I was hearing correctly. "Cut the shit, Ed. Don't fuck with me like that."

Ed said, "I am sorry to be the one to tell you, but that's what the orders say."

Silence dominated the conversation, or more aptly, the lack of conversation.

I was devastated and somewhat heartbroken. What happened, I thought. What will I do out in Brighton? Did I piss someone off?

Engine 29 was situated in the Brighton section of Boston almost completely surrounded by Brookline and Newton. The company was not very busy. Engine 29 was housed with Ladder 11 and the District 11 chief.

♪♪♪♫

In September of 1969 two of my friends and I had gone down to New York City to buff. Over the years we had developed friendships at the Brooklyn Communications Office. The C. O. in Brooklyn was within view of a housing project that was built on the site of Ebbets Field. Ebbets Field was the home of the Brooklyn Dodgers from 1890 until 1957 when the team was moved to the west coast. Los Angeles, California stole the hearts of many baseball fans. New York was home to the Dodgers, the Giants, and of course the dreaded Yankees.

On the corner of Empire Boulevard and Sullivan Place sits a magnificent stone edifice which houses the Communications Office of the borough of Brooklyn. In the sixties, it was truly an unbelievable operation. Call takers answered the phones, writing information on index cards which traveled through a belt system to the dispatcher who notified the companies to respond to alarms. When a report of a building fire was received the box was transmitted and the full first alarm response was on the road within seconds, responding to the location of the fire. In the sixties this happened thousands of times a day in the FDNY. The workload would be overwhelming for one office, so each of the five boroughs has their own Communications Office.

Brooklyn was burning in the sixties and the seventies, as was the Bronx. Every night there was at least a couple of building fires and perhaps more than just a couple.

When we visited the Brooklyn C.O. our arrival was met with one of our acquaintances which we had made over the years making a phone call. The call was placed to a fire officer from a busy company who enjoyed hosting firefighters from other cities. The call might be made to the Captain of Engine 277, the Lieutenant at Ladder 108 or the Battalion Chief of a busy battalion in the borough. After visiting and being fascinated by the volume of runs that were handled by the dispatchers, my friends and I would head out to their host firehouse to spend the night.

I was awaiting a date in December when I would be appointed to the Boston Fire Department when I made the first of many trips to the FDNY. On this very first visit I became friends with a dispatcher named Glenn Gilberg. Glenn settled in at the Brooklyn C. O. since he was not able to be appointed to the firefighting force of the FDNY since he was height challenged. For those who do not know or don't remember, an applicant had to have certain physical characteristics to be an appropriate candidate for the fire department.

For instance, your height must be in excess of five feet, four inches, your eyesight must be able to be corrected to 20/20. You must have all of your digits, both toes and fingers. Of course, your weight must be in an approved range. All of this in addition to being physically fit, healthy and able to pass an aggressive strength testing environment.

Glenn could not meet the height requirement. For a little guy he had the heart of a giant. All he wanted to do in life was to become a firefighter. Glenn even took out an ad in Fire Engineering magazine in an attempt to market himself as a firefighter.

His quest took him to Boston where he had an aunt who lived in a nice residential section of the city known as Mattapan. Glenn traveled up to Boston to take the written exam and again to take the strength test. He mentioned to me that he was going to be appointed in December to the Boston Fire Department.

"I am going on your job soon", he said with the air of a man who had finally achieved his lifelong dream.

"What do you mean?" I replied.

"I have an aunt who lives in Mattapan and I took the test using her address. I passed and I am going to be appointed in December."

I was simply amazed at this coincidental turn of events.

"Why don't you come up and stay at my house the day before our swearing-in. I'll drive so that you won't have to worry about finding anything" I said.

Glenn replied, "That would be great. I won't have to worry about finding Fire Headquarters from Mattapan."

So on December 23, 1969 Glenn arrived from the big city. He spent the day before preparing for his 'moment of a lifetime' and arrived early in the day to visit with me, my wife and our daughter, Stacey.

On the morning of Christmas Eve, Glenn and I set out for the trek to Fire Headquarters. The two of us were joined by fifty-eight other candidates at 115 Southampton Street in Roxbury. At 0900 all sixty male applicants, one of whom was black, were sworn in as FFOPs, the term used by the Boston Fire Department to describe Firefighters on Probation. The probationary period at the time was six months. Anything that you did wrong could get you fired with no further explanation and no hearing. For six months these FFOPs walked on eggshells, broke no laws, feared even getting a speeding ticket, and learned everything that was taught to them at Moon Island.

♪♪♪

Moon Island is the site of the BFD's training academy. It is situated on a plot of land that once was indeed an island in Boston Harbor. Today it is connected by a causeway to the City of Quincy, through which one must travel for a mile and a half to get into Boston. Here an FFOP traveled daily. He sat in a classroom for roll call in the morning. This was followed by outdoor evolutions, lunch and more evolutions.

A typical day at Moon Island goes like this. Roll call at 0800 by one of the Fire Lieutenant instructors. The Drillmaster, Fire Captain Dick Duffley would read you the riot act and prepare you for the day's agenda. Once outside you would throw a fifty foot ladder to one side of the burn building and a 35 foot ladder to another. Each and every FFOP would climb to the roof, cross the roof and descend from the roof over the other ground ladder. We did this in the morning, we did this after lunch and we did this before we made up the ladders just prior to dismissal.

Normally drill school lasted six or eight weeks, but this class of FFOPs was different. You might think that Christmas Eve is a strange day to appoint sixty firefighters to the department. The reason for this was quite simple. In the Boston Fire Department everything happened on a Wednesday. You were hired, promoted, transferred and suspended, if necessary, on a Wednesday. December 24th in 1969 was a Wednesday and it was the last Wednesday prior to December 29th. The importance of December 29th is that this was the day of the reduction of work hours from forty-eight to forty-six hours per week (on average). These sixty FFOPs were necessary additions to fill the roles for the needed number of bodies to fully complement the companies.

The long-awaited reduction of work hours was not come by easily. It was long overdue and the plan now was quite simple. On the final Wednesday in 1969 the work schedule was reduced to a 46 hour work week. The next year on the final Wednesday of 1970, it was planned to further reduce the average work week to a 44 hour week and then again, in 1971 the final Wednesday of the year would see the implementation of a 42 hour work week.

On paper this seemed plausible, simple and easily transitioned. One major problem was encountered. Nobody could come up with a schedule for a 44 hour work week. The city and the union mutually agreed that the membership would work an additional 6 months at 46 hours and then enter into the 42 hour week six months earlier, on the last Wednesday of June, 1971.

While this was quite a simple solution I often wondered what happened to the few individuals who retired between January and July in 1971. Didn't they work an extra two hours a week for six months? I am sure that if the same situation arose today monetary compensation would become a factor.

Section Two
Engine 29

CHAPTER 7

Assigned to Engine 29

"Engine 29, I can't believe I'm going to Engine 29", I thought to myself over and over again. While I was so wrapped in my grief about my assignment, I failed to consider the most important fact: I was going to be an FFOP in the Boston Fire Department.

FFOP is the abbreviation for 'Firefighter on Probation'. For my first six months on the job there was no union protection for an FFOP. Anything illegal or extremely stupid that you did could get you terminated with no appeal. Since my appointment the length of probationary time has been extended to one year.

On December 24th Glenn and I dressed in our chambray shirts and new dungarees, black work shoes, black socks and black belt. This was the work uniform for a firefighter in 1969. We drove together to our swearing-in at Memorial Hall at Fire Headquarters in Roxbury.

I knew several of the guys I was appointed with.

After the ceremony we drove to our assigned fire houses to see which group we would be working on and to meet the officers on duty. The next day was a holiday for us. The following Monday we reported to Moon Island for some indoctrination.

The sixty recruits or FFOPS were told that the class was being split up into three groups. I was in the third group, group 'C'. The instructor explained to us that this class was going to be a little different since we were needed in the firehouses very quickly.

Each group would report to Moon Island for two weeks, all six days at the training academy. The usual scheduling for FFOPs was Monday to Friday at Moon Island and Saturday night tours in their respective firehouses.

My group would report to the training academy in February so this meant that I would spend the next four weeks at Engine 29 in Brighton. I found out that I was being assigned to group 9.

There were five of us going to my new firehouse at 138 Chestnut Hill Avenue. Three were assigned to Engine 29 and two to Ladder 11. Of the three assigned to the engine one would eventually transfer to Ladder 6, I would go to Ladder 20 in about a year and a half. The other individual would be terminated for his role in a breaking and entering escapade.

Ladder 11's new FFOPs would have one staying there for his entire career and one transferring to Ladder 15 after about a year.

I would be working two of my three days and nights with another new guy, Blair Llewellyn. I took a liking to Blair since he was a pretty 'sparky' guy also. He was the one who would transfer to Ladder 15. While working there he would suffer a career ending injury when he climbed the aerial to a man who was threatening to jump from the YMCA on Huntington Avenue. Blair grabbed him in midair and the result was a severe injury to his arm.

When I reported to Engine 29 I had been given a fire helmet and boots. I did not yet have a fire coat. For the first couple of weeks when I worked I had to borrow one from another member. That was it! We had none of the necessary safety equipment that we are assigned today. No light, no gloves, no bunker gear, no PASS device. All of that equipment would come in due time.

I rode on the back step of an old Ward LaFrance pumper. This was a spare piece of apparatus since Engine 29's regularly assigned piece was on its way to the junk yard. Until just prior to my appointment Engine 29 had been designated as an Engine Squad. There were five engine squads scattered around the city. ES11 in East Boston, ES14 in Roxbury, ES18 in Dorchester, ES45 in Roslindale and of course good old ES29 in Brighton. Five 1947 Mack pumpers were retrofitted with compartments to be used by the squad companies. These squad pieces also had a ladder rack mounted on the roof.

The engine squads were developed after two of the three rescue companies were disbanded. They were geographically placed around the city. Just a short time before my appointment, in June and July of 1969, the City decided to disband the engine squads and return the companies to regular engine company operations. The squads had been designed to take up the slack since the city was now operating with only one Rescue Company. The rescue equipment was transferred to ladder companies in the district.

Squad 29's equipment went to Ladder 11 and Squad 45's equipment went to Ladder 16. Both of these ladder companies were in the same house as the engines.

Squad 11's equipment went to Ladder 2, Squad 14's went to Ladder 26 and Squad 18's went to Ladder 27. These three ladder trucks were nearest to the affected Engine Squads.

No more Engine Squads!

CHAPTER **8**

District 11

I would be working in District 11 for a while before I would be able to transfer to a busier company. I would make the most of it. When another group of new appointees came on the job it would open up the door for guys who had transfer requests in to make their moves and the new FFOPs would fill the slots left open.

Meantime I would get to know District 11 pretty well. The district was 98% surrounded by the Charles River, Brookline, and Newton with only a sliver of Commonwealth Avenue connecting us to the main part of Boston. Help was usually a long time coming.

Now this may seem like a large response area, but there weren't any fires back then. There was plenty of potential, but no fires. I did anything that I could to get out of the firehouse and go somewhere where something might happen.

I understand that this may seem like a ghoulish thing to wish for, a fire to occur so that I could work it. There's an old saying that I read somewhere that says, "I don't want to see anybody's house burn, but if it should, then I want to be there."

At the time of my appointment there were four firehouses with six fire companies in the district.

Engine 29 and Ladder 11 were quartered at the district headquarters with the District Chief at 138 Chestnut Hill Avenue.

Engine 41 and Ladder 14 were in the Allston section at 16 Harvard Avenue. They were the busiest companies in the district.

Engine 51 was all alone in Oak Square at 425 Faneuil Street. They had the distinction of being one of the quietest companies in the city.

Engine 34 was also in quarters by themselves at 444 Western Avenue.

In November of 1972 Ladder 22 was reassigned to the quarters of Engine 51 when a new firehouse in Charlestown was opened and Ladder 22 was deemed surplus in Charlestown and the need for another ladder company in Brighton was recognized.

Apparently the need for this additional ladder truck was no longer necessary in 1981. This is when the fire department and its members were made pawns in then Mayor Kevin H. White's political fiasco known as the Tregor Bill and Proposition 2 1/2.

Ladder 22 and Engine 34 were disbanded. They would never be in service again and the quarters of Engine 34 were sold to a private enterprise.

23 companies would be closed with only three ever being reopened. Hundreds of firefighters were laid off and dozens of fire officers demoted. Overtime was employed to hire firefighters to staff companies after hundreds were laid off.

This political maneuver had firefighters losing their homes, marriages were destroyed and many have never gotten over this wanton nonsense employed by an administration that just didn't give a damn about city workers.

Later under the leadership of Fire Commissioner/Chief of Department Leo D. Stapleton two companies would start out for District 11 upon receipt of a struck box so that some protection would remain in the district in case of a subsequent alarm of fire. Engine 37 and Ladder 26 would travel out to the quarters of Engine 41 and Ladder 14 to be available to the citizens of Brighton.

This situation called for the movement of two of the busiest companies in the city to be on the road hundreds of additional times a year besides their already busy running cards.

Today District 11 continues to have a tremendous fire potential with thousands of students and hundreds of businesses coupled with the 'normal' residential areas.

CHAPTER 9

The Chief Was Jumping Up and Down in the Street

Have you ever heard that expression? I had heard it throughout my buffing career and the short time that I had been on the job. I had never seen that character, that chief who jumped up and down, but considered it a possibility. I also knew that in reality it was just a fire-fighting expression. It was used to describe a chief who got excited when he saw black smoke and red fire.

This particular night tour was a fairly warm spring night and the evening had been an interesting, but rather frustrating one. Shortly after dinner time we had a run to the project. I was on the back step this night tour.

We were running our perpetual spare piece since we no longer had a regular piece. Our regular piece had been out of service for what seemed like an eternity. As a matter of fact I had never seen our regular fire engine yet. Engine 29 responded to this particular project fairly often, however not as often as other companies responded to other housing projects.

We took our usual, meandering route to the project. We turned right on Chestnut Hill Avenue, then right on Union Street. Next it was left on Monastery Road, and finally right on Washington

Street. As we turned left onto Fidelis Way we could smell it. The infamous odor of rubbish was the smell. Two thirds into the winding thoroughfare we came upon the source. A small outside rubbish fire was burning in a courtyard. I assisted the ever smiling Joe Benson in running a 1 ½" nuisance line and extinguishing the 'roaring inferno'.

I remembered thinking, "It wasn't much, but at least we passed water tonight".

I noticed that there wasn't much pressure in the line, but heck, I'm the new guy. After the fire was doused, Joe called for the line to be shut down. We started to drain the line and return the two pieces of 1 ½" back to the pump. As we got nearer we heard the captain and Jim, the pump operator discussing a problem with the pump.

The captain told us to run 50 feet back out because they wanted to check something.

Joe Benson and I reattached the line to the pump discharge, put the nozzle back on and waited and waited and waited some more. We got nothing but dribbles from the nozzle. Jim said that this spare piece which we had been running for months has had one problem after another. We returned to quarters and called for the Motor Squad to come out to take a look at this monster.

The Motor Squad hated coming all the way out to Brighton since it was a long trek for them. With the exception of maybe midnight to the early morning hours there was always traffic and no easy way to make the trip.

When the MS arrived they took us out to a hydrant and tried every trick in the book to get water. It was then that we heard the infamous 'shop job'. This meant that we would have to strip the piece while the MS attempted to find a spare, or should I say another spare to replace our spare. Eventually we were told that they were going to get another spare and they would be back in a while.

Meantime Ladder 11 had a few runs with other engine companies and we sat waiting. I figured, "This is it! They are going to have a fire while we sit waiting with no fire engine to respond on".

I was young and new on the job and couldn't wait for our next fire. Most of the guys I was working with couldn't care less if they ever went to another fire. Every time I would complain about sitting in quarters they would tell me to shut up and read a book or something.

Finally, the Motor Squad arrived with a spare that was almost identical to the one we had been running. We took that pump out to the hydrant and attempted to get water. We did, but Jim said that there was something funny sounding about this pump. Jimmy didn't like it but we were determined that it would have to last for the night.

An hour or so after we finished repacking the hose, the equipment and the gear we had a run for an automobile fire outside Brighton Center. We responded. The new spare started OK and it stopped OK. The siren worked and the radio worked. When we ran out our 1 ½" line to the car which was burning we actually got water. Joe extinguished the fire with me right behind him on the line. He said, "Hey kid, the next one is all yours."

We made up our line. Got on the back step, and headed for quarters. Two blocks from quarters we stopped. Joe and I looked at each other and shrugged our shoulders.

"What's going on?" we asked the chauffeur. His reply to us was, "I think it is the clutch. I think it's gone."

I couldn't believe it. It was now 11:00 pm and we were once again waiting for the Motor Squad. This time they arrived with the wrecker.

They towed Engine 29 to the firehouse where we stripped it on the apron. When we finished, off went the MS and Engine 29's spare, replacement spare.

About three quarters of an hour later they returned driving another spare which made the first two look like Cadillacs. They asked the captain to come to the main floor. When he came down the Motor Squad told him that this was the last spare piece in the city. However there was one problem. This pump could not get water. We were right back to where we had started.

Captain Tehan decided that the district chief had to know about this. He called Chief Snow down and explained the situation to him. The Motor Squad said that if we could get by until morning the original spare we had been using could be repaired and put back in service. Chief Snow decided that at any rate we could get to the fire and the manpower could use hose or other equipment from other companies.

Well at approximately 3:00 am what do you suppose happened? Fire Alarm struck a box for a building fire about seven blocks from the firehouse at the corner of Washington Street and Argus Place.

Engine 29 arrived and had fire showing from under the rear stairs. We stretched a line and waited for the next pump, Engine 51, to arrive. The District Chief said to get water on it. He was shouting at us like we were fools of some sort. Captain Tehan reminded him that this pump could not get water.

I watched as this man who had passed at least three exams and was promoted three times was literally jumping up and down in the street. He was hollering at us because we couldn't get water while screaming something about this being the most fucked up thing he had ever seen. I had to agree with him! It was!

I remembered about three hours ago he had been advised and he agreed that we would have to make do with what we had until morning. That is what was fucked up!

Please Lord, get me out of this firehouse!

CHAPTER **10**

All of the Chiefs in District 11 Were Characters

Engine 29 responded to every 5000 series box with the exception of four; Box 51, 511, 5113, and 5117. We went to the entire Brighton section of Boston minus four boxes. They had no multiple alarm running card in 1969. No matter how bad a fire was, we weren't going.

I took every detail out of the firehouse. I went to Engine 51, Engine 41, Ladder 14. Anytime I might be able to be in a better spot to catch a fire, I took it. One day Captain Tippy announced that there was a detail to Engine 53 in Roslindale. I told him that I'd take it. Engine 53 was first due to my house and the commute home would be shorter than from Brighton. Besides, Engine 53 moved on every second alarm in the city.

Well, as luck would have it, there *was* a fire that day, in Brighton. I had outsmarted myself again. Engine 29 was second due, but they arrived without me.

❧❧❧❧

Another task that I volunteered for was the fill-in chief's aide. I covered vacations on my group when Joe 'Jelly' Ceurvels was on vacation or off injured. Not only that, I told the captain that I would cover all of the aides' vacations. This would mean a group change when I covered the others, but it was a great opportunity to see how the other groups worked.

The chief that I covered most often, Chief Snow, was on group 8. District Chief Bill Pineo was on group 5. He was one of the most colorful characters that I had met on the job in my few short months. Bernie Pritchard was his regular aide and I covered his vacations also.

Bernie had been a firefighter on Engine 10 when Pineo was the captain there. A district chief gets to choose his own aide and Pineo took Bernie with him when he made district chief and was assigned to District 11.

Chief Pineo knew just about every regular resident of Brighton with the exception of about four. When I say regular resident, I mean except the students who changed every four years. After we made our rounds to the other three firehouses we would travel around the district and say hello to just about everyone.

$$\text{⠒⠒⠒}$$

Every morning the district chief would make the rounds. We would travel to Engine 51 and then to Engine 34 and finally stop at Engine 41. At each firehouse the chief would be met by the officer who would bring down the outgoing papers which would eventually end up at Fire Headquarters.

When we got to Engine 51 I would pull onto the apron in front of the overhead doors. Pineo would not go inside at Engine 51 since he hated the officer who worked here on his group. It was my responsibility to enter the firehouse and get the papers which were usually left at the patrol desk area. The lieutenant would leave the papers there just in case the chief decided to make entry into these uncharted waters.

Chief Pineo's favorite stop would be at Engine 34. We might spend a good amount of time here as he chatted each day.

When we arrived at Engine 41 we would be met by a character who was a lieutenant on Ladder 14 named Gerry Walton. Walton's nickname was 'Stony'. He was as much a character as Chief Pineo and there was only room for one character in Brighton on group 5.

◢◢◢◣

One afternoon when I was driving DFC Bill Pineo, we were responding to Box 5288 located at Birmingham Parkway and Lincoln Street. As we approached Market Street in Brighton Center we could see a cloud of black smoke on the horizon.

Ladder 14 entered the intersection ahead of us from North Beacon Street to Market Street. Lieutenant 'Stony' Walton called off and ordered a 'working fire'. Chief Pineo did not like being one-upped at his fires. His direction to me was, "Block that working fire".

This was something that was not often done on the radio. It usually has embarrassing results. I called Fire Alarm and told them that "Car 11 is on scene. Hold that."

The reply from Fire Alarm was, "OK Car 11 you are at 5288. We'll hold the working fire."

Pineo jumped out of the district car, he ran around to the rear of the building sans fire gear. When he ran back out front I spotted him. When he saw me he held up two fingers thereby signifying that he wanted a second alarm.

Later when lieutenant Walton was talking to me, he asked, "What is wrong with that guy?"

I said, "I don't know. Maybe he just doesn't like you."

Then I ducked as Walton swung at me.

❧❧❧

Every night we would stop at the chief's house for a bite to eat. His wife was the loveliest lady that you could ever want to meet. She was so sweet and kind. They made a most unlikely couple. Pineo was gruff and loud. He enjoyed a good confrontation.

One night as we sat at their kitchen table, I was reading the paper and the chief went down to the cellar. A few minutes after his descent to his man cave I heard two or three gunshots.

"Oh my God, he just offed himself in the basement", I thought.

Mrs. Pineo came into the kitchen just as I put the newspaper down and started to go to the basement to check on him. She informed me that the noise was just Bill shooting his pistol down there in his home-made shooting range in the cellar.

Nice going, Bill. I just shit my pants thinking that you went to the 'big fire district in the sky'.

I enjoyed driving Pineo, a true character if there ever was one.

Many years later I was acting captain at Engine 5 in East Boston. The chief over there was Harry Daniels. Daniels was the ex-husband of Pineo's daughter. While I was there at Engine 5, Bill Pineo passed away.

Mrs. Pineo called Harry and asked if he had a spare sack coat to bury Bill in. Harry Daniels said, "Boy, wouldn't Bill roll over in his grave if he knew he would be wearing my uniform."

R. I. P. Bill, you were something else.

۸۸۸

The DFC on my group was Chief Snow, another character, a strange character. This same man was described in the previous chapter. He lived his entire life by the clock. He ate by the clock, made his rounds by the clock and I think he even took a crap by the clock and nothing had better interfere.

When we went out in the morning we would go to the firehouses and after Engine 41 the next stop was always to the State Fire Marshal's Office at 1010 Commonwealth Avenue. When we arrived there the aide would go to the second floor and drop off the auto fire cards from the previous day.

These were pre-computer days. Then again 1999 was pre-computer days in the BFD. Every DFC had to make out what was then known as an automobile fire card. These cards would be sent to District 11 and the next working day the DFC would deliver them to the State Fire Marshal's Office.

After we left 1010 we would head back to the firehouse for the rest of the day awaiting the clock to signify that it was time to go home.

Night tours were as equally fascinating. During the night tour, papers coming *from* fire headquarters needed to be delivered to the various firehouses in the district.

After the 6 pm news and weather, this DFC would call me down to the main floor and we would make the rounds with any orders, or other important paperwork to be delivered to Engine 51, 34 and 41's quarters.

My favorite day while driving this chief was Friday, fish day. The route for Fridays was to leave our firehouse and head to Engine 51. From there we would next stop at Engine 34. The next stop after Engine 34 was at the dry cleaners in Allston for the uniforms. After that stop it was to the Chinese hand laundry on Franklin Street where the white uniform shirts would be waiting. From there we went to Engine 41 and then to 1010 Commonwealth Avenue with the auto cards.

Since we were on the district and city line, we would cut across Babcock Street into Brookline. Next stop: Wulf's Fish Market on Harvard Street in Brookline. After the fish market it was just a few short blocks and we were back in Brighton. Next stop was to Chief Snow's house to drop off the dry cleaning, white shirts, and the fish.

But wait, the day was not over yet. At some precise time around 3:00 pm we had to go to the chief's house again and put the fish in the oven, set the timer and then return to the district headquarters to await the arrival of the chief's relief.

One day as our trip around the district was about to begin one of the guys asked me if I would stop at an auto parts store and pick up an alternator for him so that he could replace his later in the day. I had absolutely no problem making this stop, but you should have heard the chief when I stopped at the auto parts store. He thought that was ridiculous that he had to wait while I did an errand for one of the guys.

When I returned with the alternator I told Jim Melia that in the future he would have to check with the almighty chief to see if we could squeeze in his errand between the dry cleaners, the laundry and the fish market.

❧❧❧

One more chief that I was the fill-in aide for was Chief Dunn. He also lived in the district. He was a very quiet man with a personality of a toad. We made our rounds in the district and hardly eight words were ever spoken between us.

At noontime he would direct me to go to his house so that he could eat his lunch with his wife. He told me that I could park down the street under a shady tree and that he wouldn't be too long. Now I had long ago found out that 'not too long' was a matter of interpretation. My idea of 'not too long' is fifteen or so minutes, his was 45 minutes.

We only were on the road for as long as department business would require of us.

CHAPTER 11

Brighton Characters

There were as many characters in Brighton as well as in any other district in the city.

I worked with John 'John Joe' McHugh. He was on my group, but on the ladder truck, Ladder 11. John Joe told me about how the old ladder truck's rear wheels would fit right into the streetcar tracks that ran through Brighton.

Today's ladder trucks have a permanent steering system. In the old ladder trucks the tiller man used to sit up on top of the wooden aerial and the steering spindle went down and was threaded through the aerial and the ground ladders. It then sat in the steering box mechanism. The end of the spindle had a groove which interlocked into the steering box and thereby you could steer the rear wheels. When the ladder truck arrived at a fire the first thing that the tiller man did was throw the tiller seat, swing the windshield out of the way and remove the spindle.

One day when he was tillering, the rear wheels fell into the streetcar tracks and when he attempted to steer out of the tracks the tiller wheel spindle came up out of the groove that it sat in. For a short distance the ladder trucks rear wheels were steering themselves. Thank God the chauffeur didn't turn off of Washington Street before John Joe was able to reinsert the spindle into the steering box.

Fifty Cent Haircuts

John Joe was also a barber. He would come into the firehouse carrying his little black bag of tools for haircuts. The cellar of Engine 29 was outfitted with a real authentic barber chair. You could get a haircut for fifty cents.

One Ball

Francis D. was riding the back step of Engine 29 when the company was involved in a serious accident. The pumper tipped over in Brighton Center. Frank had serious injuries and was hospitalized. The accident resulted in Frank having one of his testicles removed. Ole 'One ball' was able to return to work and finish out his career.

Don't Sleep in ~~My~~ His Bed

Another Brighton character was Henry J. Henry was the sole occupant of a tiny room off of the bunk room. His bed was in there since no one would allow him to sleep in any of the other bunks for reasons that I will leave to the imagination.

The Dancer

Tom M. was 'The Dancer'. He and Henry B. would go dancing every Friday night at a local dance hall in search of ladies.

My Mentor

Jim Melia was the senior man on my group. He took me under his wing. I was supposed to shadow him in the firehouse and on the company according to the captain. Jim was a great guy and a bull at a fire. Living a dozen or so blocks from the firehouse kept him in Brighton on Engine 29 for his entire career.

Brrr. It's Cold Out There.

One certain chief's driver would never get out of the car. This was in the days before portable radios. If the chief wanted him to send a message to Fire Alarm, he would send one of us over to give the message to his driver. Jimmy would crank the window down about an inch and a half to hear what you had to say. He was really a very good fellow.

Paul O'Brien

Paul was a firefighter on Ladder 11 when I was there. Shortly after my appointment Paul finished high on the lieutenant's exam and was promoted to lieutenant a short time later. Paul went to Engine 22 as a lieutenant and spent the rest of his career there. These were the only two companies for Paul in his thirty odd years on the job.

Jim Galvin

Jim studied with Paul and the two of them were promoted off of the same list. Both Jim and Paul O'Brien had previously been members of the Boston Protective Department. The protective was a company which did salvage work at commercial buildings which were struck by fire or where sprinklers were activated. They were funded by the insurance companies and acted to prevent water damage. Jimmy went to Ladder 28 as a lieutenant and as with Paul O'Brien he only served on two companies for his entire career.

CHAPTER 12

I've Done My Time

After close to eighteen months in the purgatory known as District 11, I knew that I had to move on. There were busier places to be and I just wasn't learning anything here. I was twenty four years old and anxious to become a better firefighter. In the fire service you get better at what you do by doing it more often. You also learn by working with firefighters who have a lot of fire experience.

I had submitted a transfer paper requesting a transfer to Ladder 20. I felt that the time was right for a spot in the firehouse where I had 'sparked' for years. At the time there was no seniority system for transfers. A few months went by and nothing happened.

One day as I was visiting my parents, my father and I had a talk about my desire to get out of Brighton. My dad asked me if I wanted him to make a call.

"A call", I said, "To whom?"

He told me not to be concerned, but if I needed help he might know someone who could help.

My dad was a chef in a restaurant in Roslindale. It was a combination bar/restaurant called Flynn's Steak House on Centre Street. Since it was a section of the city where politicians and many influential people stopped by it was not unusual for him to 'know' people.

He would come home many nights with Red Sox tickets, tickets for shows, trade shows and numerous other events. Many of the regulars were contractors with the city and others had 'in tight' connections.

❧❧❧

A few days later I received a call from a high ranking officer from Fire Headquarters who said that he heard that I was interested in a transfer.

My reply was "Yes, Sir. I am ready to move on to a busier company."

He asked where I wanted to go. When I said that I would love to go to Ladder 20 his answer was, "That's a tough place to get into."

"Where else would you consider?" he asked.

I said with no hesitation, "Engine 43".

He chuckled and replied, "I meant what other house?"

I thought for a moment and answered, "I guess any house in Dorchester or Roxbury, but I would really love to get into Ladder 20".

He told me to sit tight and give him a week or two to see what he could do for me. He also told me to put in a Form 5 requesting a transfer. I reminded him that I did that about six months ago. At this point he advised me that there was no paper at headquarters from me requesting a transfer. My immediate thoughts went to Captain Tippy and his reputation for not forwarding transfer requests.

Some captains are unscrupulous. They feel as though it looks bad upon their position as a captain if a lot of young firefighters are looking to get out of their company. My original paper had disappeared between Engine 29 and Fire Headquarters. He had a reputation for just this sort of thing. I had been warned.

The next day tour when I presented my new paper for him to sign (again), his reply was, "You already put a paper in. I felt compelled to say that I had someone look into it and nothing could be found.

Three or four days later this gentleman from headquarters called me again. This time he said, "Richard, you are in luck. There happens to be a firefighter at Ladder 20 who is interested in going to Fire Prevention." He told me that it might be a few weeks.

I was so ready and anxious I actually had the balls to ask him if I could get a permanent detail to Ladder 20.

He said that "They don't really like to do that anymore. Just sit tight. You'll be there soon, kid."

I told him that "I was lucky to have been able to have somebody like him to help me out".

I thanked him over and over.

Wow, is this really happening? I couldn't wait. It was like being appointed to a new job again. This is going to be better than going to Ladder 4.

◆◆◆

The next day I went to work at Engine 29. I read the orders that had come out over the last few days. There was nothing about transfers. My heart sunk a little bit. I remembered, "Just sit tight."

The following day I worked the night tour. In the evening the orders were received and 'Lo and behold!', there it was!

FF Michael J. Connolly   Ladder 20   to   Fire Prevention Division

FF Richard Connelly   Engine 29   to   Ladder 20

It was right in front of me, in writing, and I still couldn't believe it.

I packed up my stuff from my upstairs locker and in the morning I removed my fire gear from my downstairs locker. I said goodbye to the guys who had broken me in.

I left with a tear in my eye since this had been my first assignment on the Boston Fire Department. I certainly hadn't been too crazy about being here, but I was a Boston Firefighter and I would be for 40 more years.

Section Three
Ladder 20

CHAPTER 13

Engine 43 and Ladder 20

The very first firehouse that I ever set foot into was at 5 Boston Street in Andrew Square, South Boston. My dad took me to see the fire station. It was probably around 1953 and I would have been 6 or 7 years old. This was the home of Engine 43 and Ladder 20. They were the first due companies to my house while I was growing up.

My mother used to walk me up to shop at the stores on West Broadway in Southie. We would pass Engine 1's quarters at 119 Dorchester Street and I would stand on the concrete bumpers outside the doors and look in at the fire engines. I remember that the firehouse had dutch doors and even though the bottom would be closed I could still peer into the open top half. Of course on the return trip I would have to do it all over again.

When I was a senior at Boston English High School a classmate and friend of mine, Steve Dalton, brought me into Engine 43 and Ladder 20 after they had moved to a new location at 920 Massachusetts Avenue. Steve knew the captain of Engine 43 since Captain Bob Regan was the father of Steve's girlfriend, Carolyn.

This was a life changing event for me. The evening that I spent there became the start of a relationship that molded my entire life. I met Captain Bob and Lieutenant Jim Kennedy of Ladder 20.

When the house alarm sounded Captain Regan told me to hop on Ladder 20 with Lieutenant Kennedy. He took Steve with him on Engine 43. I continued to stop in and spend some time at this firehouse as a 'spark'. I was often invited to ride with either company. Eventually this arrangement lasted about six years doing this a couple of nights a week.

When I first was sparking at Engine 43 they were assigned an old 1952 Pirsch pumper which was the last Pirsch fire apparatus purchased by the City of Boston. Shortly after I began sparking here Engine 43 would receive a new 1964 Ward LaFrance pump. This was the final open cab fire apparatus assigned to the company. These pieces were followed by a 1968 Ward LaFrance, a 1970 Hahn, and a 1974 Ward LaFrance pumper.

The 1974 Ward La France pump would be the final pump ever assigned to Engine 43. There were five of these 1974 Wards and they were assigned to Engine Company 16, 17, 24, 43 and 53.

Ladder 20 had been running a 1949 Pirsch ladder truck. In 1963, just before I began my sparking career, they received an open cab 1963 Ward LaFrance tractor to draw an older American LaFrance 85 foot wooden aerial. Ladder 20 ran this truck until 1968 when they received a new American LaFrance closed cab 100 foot metal aerial. This is the truck that was in service when I transferred into the firehouse in 1971.

In 1972 the company assumed possession of a new 1972 Maxim ladder truck, tractor drawn, with a 100 foot metal aerial. This was the best truck I ever served on. It was a pleasure to drive. The stick flew out of the bed and the fly sections extended quickly.

The aerial had a feature called 'Top-Trol' which allowed a member at the tip to move the aerial left or right. It was rarely, if ever, used.

The 1972 Maxim was followed by a 1976 Seagrave 100 foot, tractor drawn aerial which would be the final truck ever assigned to Ladder 20. All of these last three trucks assigned to Ladder 20 had enclosed tiller seats.

The city bought eight of these Seagrave trucks. They were assigned to Ladder companies 4, 7, 10, 11, 13, 20, 23, and 29. Another note of significance here is that these trucks were the final tractor drawn aerials or 'tiller trucks' to be purchased by the City of Boston.

♪♪♪

My transfer brought me to Ladder 20 in another chapter in my life. No longer was I a visitor or a 'spark' here. This was going to be my firehouse. I worked here now. This was truly a dream come true for me.

My first assignment was to group one. I would be working with some great guys here and the boss would be Lieutenant Jim Dailey.

After Christmas, 1971 I was informed that I would be going to group three. This was going to be my regular group, or as regular as regular might get. There was one thing that I didn't like about group three, but I can work through anything and anybody. Things change, don't they?

My officer on group three was Lieutenant Paul McNiff. Lieutenant McNiff was one of those characters that I describe again and again in my tales. He was a good guy, a good firefighter, and a good boss.

♪♪♪

Engine 43 and Ladder 20 was a unique firehouse. Almost every response from this station involved a left turn from the firehouse except to one box and one street.

Department-wise the firehouse was in District 6 (South Boston) and

Division I. It was geographically in Roxbury. The companies responded to Districts 4, 5, 6, 7 and 13.

This newer firehouse had been constructed in 1951 as part of the new Fire Department Headquarters and Maintenance Shops complex. In addition to the administrative part of the complex there was also a fire station built for Engine Company 23 and Lighting Plant 2.

On July 13, 1954 Engine 23 was disbanded and the Lighting Plant was moved to the Quarters of Engine 3 at 618 Harrison Avenue in the South End.

The firehouse at 900 Massachusetts Avenue sat unoccupied for a few years and became a natural location when it became apparent that the firehouse in Andrew Square needed to be replaced. It had been built in 1898.

On July 1, 1961 the Andrew Square firehouse, situated at 5 Boston Street, was closed and the companies were relocated to 900 Massachusetts Avenue.

On June 6, 1962 the address of the firehouse was changed to 920 Massachusetts Avenue since the address of the Maintenance Shop was also 900 Massachusetts Avenue.

Both Engine 43 and Ladder 20 were always thought of as South Boston companies since they were always in District 6 and still were. Both companies had great running cards and Ladder 20 showed up at most major fires. When five alarms were struck for a fire the response brought 19 engines, but only 5 ladder trucks. Engine 43 responded all over the city on multiple alarm fires. Ladder 20 responded to all of South Boston, a great part of Roxbury and Dorchester, the South End and downtown fires.

Another unusual feature of this firehouse was that while we were located in District 6, Division One once you went out the door and crossed the street you were in District 5, Division Two.

When the companies were relocated to Mass Avenue the running cards were changed very little with the exception of the first alarm responses. Surprisingly the companies responded almost two miles to the City Point section of South Boston, but only a few blocks into Roxbury or the South End.

One reason for this is that there were only a few fire stations in South Boston which was a peninsula. The response was basically from one direction. In the South End and Roxbury there were quite a few fire stations and the responses came from a 360° area.

Ladder 20 was either the fourth or fifth busiest ladder truck every year when I was assigned there. The other busy ladder companies were Ladder 7, Ladder 23, Ladder 4 and Ladder 30.

CHAPTER 14

The Firefighting Finn Family

My best friend was on group 3 and we would work together until Ladder 20 was closed on February 4, 1981. Paul Finn was a member of the Finn Firefighting Family. Paul's grandfather was a firefighter as was his dad, Fred Finn Sr. Fred was assigned to Engine 50 in Charlestown when he was appointed and later transferred to Engine 21 in Dorchester. This firehouse was within walking distance of the family homestead. Fred spent the remaining years of his career on Engine 21.

Paul was the first of three sons appointed to the Boston Fire Department. He was appointed in February of 1969 and was assigned to Ladder 20.

His brother Tom was next. He was assigned to Engine 17, also in Dorchester. He later transferred across the floor to Ladder 7.

Next was Paul's brother, Freddie. Fred Jr. was the youngest brother and he was appointed to Ladder 15 in the Back Bay. Freddie was a victim of the layoffs in 1981. When he was rehired after the layoffs he went back to Ladder 15 and a short time later transferred to Ladder 17 in the South End. Sometime later he transferred to Ladder 18 in South Boston.

Both Paul and Freddie were promoted to Fire Lieutenant. Paul was promoted out of Engine 21 and went on to Engine 56, Ladder 1, Engine 33, The Comm. Unit and Engine 8 as a lieutenant.

Freddie was promoted out of Ladder 18 and went back to Ladder 17 as a lieutenant.

A great family portrait sits in the home of the matriarch of the Finn Family. Years ago it was the home of the four firefighting Finns and this portrait shows all of the Finn firefighters.

Fred Sr. passed away during our stint at Ladder 20. He was a victim of one of the career sicknesses known to affect many more like him, cancer. Tommy Finn also died from that dreaded disease on February 4, 2000 while a member of Rescue Company 1. Fred Jr. is now retired from a debilitating injury he received while a Fire Lieutenant on Ladder 17. Paul retired in March of 2010 after 41 years service.

♪♪♪

There are many stories that Paul and I share as driver and tillerman on Ladder 20 from 1971 until 1981. We went to hundreds of fires together and then there were the few he missed while on vacation.

They say that when two people work together for an extended period of time they begin to think alike. They know what the other is thinking. This has never been truer than the time tested relationship between Paul Finn and Rick Connelly working together on Ladder 20.

The friendship began as early as the seventh grade at the William E. Russell School in Dorchester. We were both members of the BFD Auxiliary Engine Company CD-10. Both of us are FDNY buffs and have made numerous trips to the Big Apple. The friendship continues today and now has lasted 55 years.

I know you'll always have my back Good Friend.

CHAPTER 15

Lieutenant Jim Dailey

Jim Dailey was my first lieutenant on Ladder 20. Jim had been around for quite some time. I am not sure, but I don't ever remember seeing him smile.

Back in the early seventies the officers were still wearing white dress shirts when they worked. Why white you ask? I don't have a clue, but somewhere along the line someone decided that this would distinguish the officers from the firefighters. I don't have to tell you how long a white shirt lasted when working on a busy company. At least the FDNY had enough sense to dress their officers in grey shirts.

Jim Dailey always amazed the guys. He would arrive for work dressed in a spiffy clean and pressed white shirt under his top coat. He looked like he belonged in Esquire magazine. He would promptly head upstairs to his locker and remove his street apparel. He would then don the grungiest, graying, white shirt that you ever saw in your life. Apparently Jim never threw out any old white shirts. But rather saved them as 'work shirts'. Oh, by the way, he stored them rolled in a ball in his locker.

Lieutenant Dailey hated the Columbia Point project more than most of us. One day Ladder 20 was at another housing project in Roxbury. The name of this project was Orchard Park. Now doesn't that sound like a lovely place to live, Orchard Park.

There were no seven story buildings in Orchard Park. There were more murders in Orchard Park than there were in Columbia Point though. There was no orchard in Orchard Park either.

The streets in Orchard Park were named after battles in World War II since this project was built for the returning veterans of WW II. Bataan Ct. and Corregidor Ct., were some of the streets. Singer Bobby Brown came from the mean streets of the Orchard Park project.

The incident that we were at was concluded and the members of Ladder 20 were heading back to our ladder truck. Fire Alarm came on the air and called Ladder 20. I was the closest to the apparatus and I jumped up in the front seat and answered the radio. They gave us another response, this one to Columbia Point. I acknowledged on the radio since I was the only one near the rig.

This was long before the days of portable radios. If you weren't near the apparatus then you probably wouldn't hear the radio when the Fire Alarm Office called you.

When Lieut. Dailey realized what had happened he was pretty pissed. First of all the next run was to Columbia Point, which he despised. Secondly, he wanted to know what I was doing answering the radio when I was not in the front seat driving. He did not want to hear my explanation, as weak as it was. I realized that the best thing to do was to apologize and promise him and myself that it would never happen again. It never did happen again when I worked with Jim Dailey.

In the early morning hours whenever we responded to Columbia

Point Lieut. Dailey had a habit of hollering and banging on things since he figured that everyone who lived there was responsible for whatever reason brought us there. Jim Dailey figured that if we were up then everyone else should be too.

CHAPTER 16

Drive or Tiller?

One evening we responded to a fire on Hampden Street in Roxbury. This particular fire was in a three story brick attached residential building. It was a somewhat ordinary fire, however we had two members injured at this fire and they were both transported to the hospital.

One of these members was our tillerman, Steve McLaughlin. When the fire was knocked down and we had made up all of our equipment, Paul said to me, "What do you want to do? Do you want to drive or tiller?"

I hadn't been on the company long enough to attempt to do either one yet. My life-long dream to tiller a ladder truck was now looking me in the face.

I told Paul that I would attempt to tiller. He said that he would take it easy on me and at least get us back to the firehouse.

Well there was no problem on our return route to the firehouse, but once we arrived there the fun began.

As we pulled up out in front of the firehouse Paul remained on our side of the street until the flow of traffic abated. Then he pulled across the street with the trailer sort of diagonally in front of the doors.

This was my moment of truth, my first attempt at backing in. At this precise moment the warning tone sounded on the radio and Fire Alarm struck a box deep into South Boston.

Trial by fire! Here we go with my first run as the tillerman and I had no practice. No slowly rolling, cornering, backing up, backing in or even going straight. this was the first time that my ass was in the tiller seat and we were going about as far as we could possibly go on the first alarm. I suppose that it doesn't matter if you go 5 blocks or five miles as long as you are going straight.

I had ridden behind Paul dozens of times in the jump seat and certainly knew what a great chauffeur he was. I just hoped that he remembered that it was me back there in the tiller seat.

He did! We traveled through the streets of Southie at a safe speed and he gave me wide corners whenever he could. He must have remembered that it was his license we were driving on.

As we arrived at the location it had been determined that the fire could be handled with one and one, one engine and one ladder truck. The District Chief told us that were all set and could return. Luckily we did not have to back out of the street since we had stopped at the corner of the cross street.

OK, let's head home, I thought. I need to face the reverse devil again when we get back to quarters. Let's get this over with. There is only *one* first time.

The trip back to the firehouse was uneventful. I was sitting there realizing how much I was enjoying this assignment. I was ready, or so I thought.

Once again as we arrived at the firehouse, Paul pulled up on our side and stopped for the traffic and then he pulled across Mass. Ave. This put me in somewhat of the proper positioning for my big trip backwards.

When the driver is backing up and you are tillering, the wheel must be turned in the opposite direction that you want the trailer to move in. Naturally as we started moving in reverse, my end was heading for the engine's apparatus bay door. Paul stopped the truck and hollered to me that he would prefer it if I would put my end in the ladder truck's bay.

He pulled forward and then I realized the error of my ways. As I became familiar with the action, the trailer actually did what I wanted it to and I soon found out that it wasn't really as hard as it looked.

As the entire truck landed in the proper bay everyone got off and we surveyed the damage. The truck was fairly straight in the correct bay, there were no dents, scrapes, or scratches and the lieutenant and Paul were both happy with the result.

Hey, we were still short a guy. The two lieutenants decided that the fourth man on the engine would be detailed to Ladder 20 for the remainder of the tour. I was going to tiller for the tour.

This was actually the beginning of my nine years of tillering Ladder 20 on group 3. When Steve came back to full duty he was only with us for a very short time since he had passed the lieutenant's exam and had finished fairly high on the list. Within weeks he was out acting, as we say.

Out acting has nothing to do with being on a stage. It means that there is a temporary vacancy for an officer on a company. This officer's spot is filled with an acting lieutenant or acting captain. These acting positions are filled from the civil service list for promotion.

Steve went out acting and never returned to Ladder 20, group 3. He was promoted within months and went on to his new assignment, Ladder 29.

I continued tillering behind Paul and did so for many years.

CHAPTER 17

The Hotel Vendome Tragedy

Saturday June 17, 1972 was my father's birthday. He was turning sixty. Imagine sixty years old! Back then it was inconceivable that he was sixty years old. Today I have to look back seven years to remember what it felt like to turn sixty.

I had worked the night tour Friday night. I was home resting before I took my family over to my parents' house for cake and ice cream to celebrate.

During the late afternoon my telephone rang and it was my father asking me if I was watching the Red Sox game on television. I told him that I wasn't since I had been taking a little nap before we came to see him and my mother.

He informed me that the television cameras keep panning over the right center field wall to a fire that was burning in the Back Bay. He was wondering if I knew what was burning. I had to tell him that I had no idea, but that I would turn on my radio now that I was awake.

Shortly after I was listening to this fire I realized that it was now a fifth alarm fire with a major building collapse. Firefighters were trapped, some feared dead.

129 ❧

The Hotel Vendome was the Grand Dame of hotels built in 1872. An addition was made to the original building in 1881. Alterations were made to floor 1 in 1890. A sun parlor was added to the roof in 1911.

Even as economic times worsened the Hotel Vendome was much in demand for weddings, proms, and other social functions.

Finally bad times befell upon the Vendome. The Grand Dame suddenly fell to disrepair. Its license to operate as a hotel was revoked.

A number of fires, of both undetermined and suspicious causes, occurred between 1968 and 1971.

There were fires on January 16, 1968

April, 1968

August 1, 1968

August 3, 1968

June of 1969 saw a three alarm fire

December 27, 1969 a two alarm fire

December 31, 1969 caused more damage.

March 3, 1971 was the date of the purchase of the Hotel Vendome property by a development company. Plans called for a café, a shopping boutique and construction of 124 units of residential housing.

On December 7, 1971 the Café Vendome opened for business. Construction continued above with the continuance of the plans for shops and residential units.

During the afternoon of Saturday June 17, 1972, while diners ate at the Café, workers discovered smoke on the upper floors. Access to the areas above floor three was not readily available since the stairs had been sealed off by plywood partitions.

Investigating construction workers were unable to gain access to determine the cause of the smoke. Someone pulled fire alarm box 1571 located at Dartmouth and Newbury Streets just a block to the rear of the hotel.

Engine 33 and Ladder 15 responded from their firehouse some six blocks away. When they arrived they called off with 'light smoke showing from the fourth floor in the rear'.

The balance of the first alarm assignment arrived (two more engines and another ladder truck with the district chief) and went to work. In short fashion it was realized by the Incident Commander that the fire was much more serious than originally thought. The companies also had access issues to deal with.

The box had been received at 1435 hours and a 'Working Fire' was transmitted at 1444 hours. This 'working fire' called for an additional engine, an additional ladder truck and the Rescue Company along with the Deputy Chief of Division One.

At 1446 hours a second alarm was transmitted followed by the third alarm at 1502 hours at which time the Deputy also ordered an extra ladder company. The fourth alarm was transmitted at 1506 hours along with a request at 1552 hours for two additional engine companies.

Quite a while after the arrival of all the requested companies the members got a pretty good hold on the fire and knocked it down fairly rapidly.

The night crews were starting to arrive to relieve the day groups and the Deputy was beginning to make up some of the third and fourth alarm companies.

Suddenly 'Without Warning' at 1728 hours the southeast corner of the building collapsed. The collapse took all six floors of the building down. Many of the floors contained firefighters. Ladder 15's 1972 Maxim ladder truck was crushed and buried. Some firefighters were missing and others were feared dead.

The Deputy struck a fifth alarm and ordered the Rescue-Pumper from Division Two and the City of Cambridge Rescue Company.

The search for trapped members continued until 0245 hours the next day, Fathers' Day when the last unaccounted for member was removed.

The catastrophic result was nine members perished. Eight widows and 23 children were left without husbands and fathers. This was the worst fire in terms of loss of life of firefighters in the history of the Boston Fire Department.

The casualties were:

F. Lieut. Thomas J. Carroll	Engine 32
F. Lieut. John E. Hanbury	Ladder 13
F. F. Charles E. Dolan	Ladder 13
F. F. Joseph P. Saniuk	Ladder 13
F. F. John E. Jameson	Engine 22
F. F. Thomas W. Beckwith	Engine 32
F. F. Paul J. Murphy	Engine 32
F. F. Richard B. Magee	Engine 33
F. F. Joseph F. Boucher, Jr.	Engine 22

Joe Saniuk was the only unmarried member and Joe Boucher's wife was pregnant at the time. Joe Boucher's son is today a member of the BFD.

❧❧❧❧

Today a monument sits at the corner of Commonwealth Avenue and Dartmouth Street to honor these nine dedicated members of the Boston Fire Department who selflessly gave their lives for the citizens of Boston.

It is a semi-circular polished black granite memorial with a time line of the fire. Over the top of one part of the monument sits a replica fire coat and fire helmet of the type used in 1972. These articles look so realistic one might feel as though you could pick them up and put them on.

This most beautiful memorial is dedicated to these nine brave men and it sits in the shadow of the Hotel Vendome. It took Boston fire-fighters Local 718 twenty five years to finally attain their goal of a lasting tribute to our firefighters lost at the Vendome. We met road blocks constantly while trying to achieve our goal, but persistence paid off when on June 17, 1997 we hosted a gala of a celebration with hundreds of firefighters, guests, and a few speakers gathered for the unveiling.

❧❧❧❧

Brothers, Rest in Peace knowing that we have never forgotten!

CHAPTER **18**

My Special Vacation

In 1975 Chief HFJD was the District Chief in charge of vacations. At this point in time the district chiefs rotated on a year-to-year basis having responsibility for the vacation schedule. My wife was pregnant and due around April 26th.

I waited one morning until the arrival of the chief who was in charge of vacations this year. I intentionally waited until two weeks before my daughter Pam was born to ask for a special vacation. I was somewhat superstitious and didn't want to chance anything. I figured that by waiting until after the birth I could be home with my other two daughters for a week or so. I mean, how many people could be looking for the last week of April for vacation?

After waiting for an hour and a half, I approached the chief as he arrived at the firehouse on his morning rounds of the district.

I said good morning and informed him that I was waiting to see him.

"Chief", I said. "I was wondering if I could be granted a special vacation since my wife is due to give birth in a few weeks?"

His reply to my request was, "You've known about this for nine months. Why did you wait until now to request a special vacation?"

I was surprised at his response. I then said, "Never mind Chief, I can always swap a few tours."

"No, I'll approve it, but next time put your request in earlier", came his answer to my request.

He just hadda bust my balls!

CHAPTER **19**

Tales from the Columbia Point Project

In 1954 the Columbia Point housing project opened and the first of 1499 low income families moved in. On a forty acre site sits 15 seven story buildings and 12 three story buildings. Only the seven story buildings have the dreaded bane to firefighters: project elevators.

I would not ever be able to estimate how many times Ladder 20 responded to this one housing project never mind the other four that we responded to on first alarms.

The streets include Mt. Vernon St., Monticello Avenue, Montpelier Rd., Brandon Avenue, Belvoir Rd, and Blair Rd. These were the infamous 181 through 1817 series of boxes.

At the higher end of Monticello Avenue sits a group of seven story buildings dedicated to occupancy by seniors. These buildings are a tremendous contrast to the rest of the project.

Crime is rampant in this 'neighborhood'. In the late seventies emergency service personnel, fire and EMS, wouldn't enter the area without a police escort.

Rubbish fires, dumpster fires, automobile fires, medicals, elevator incidents, and of course, apartment fires kept us running to Columbia Point.

Vacant apartments were countless and the residents of the project enjoyed the excitement of seeing the companies respond in to fire or smoke showing. Oh, did I mention that most of these fires were on the 5th, 6th, or 7th floors?

There was never a fire where more than one line was necessary. Usually the companies took a pasting stretching lines and crawling down hallways to the fire in the rear bedroom of the apartment. As often as not the floors were littered with feces, rubbish and hypodermic needles.

Engines 21 and 43 were adept at stretching lines to the upper floors. One member would run up the stairs to a window one floor below the fire floor and drop a hauling line out of the hallway window. The other firefighters on the ground would attach the hauling line to the nozzle. When this was completed the member at the window would start hauling the line up while the other guys joined the truckies on the climb up to the fire floor.

Many times the doors to these vacant apartments would be locked, but at most incidents forcible entry was not necessary since no one had keys to lock the doors behind them after the fire was lit. Rowdy bunches of thugs would gather unused furniture and other rubbish and carry it up to the unoccupied apartment for fuel for their handiwork. They would then hang around in the street awaiting the arrival of the 'firemans'.

If some of the junk wasn't placed in an apartment, it might be taken to the roof where it could be used as munitions to bombard the arriving firefighters and police responding to the fire.

Weapons of choice included stones, bottles, and flattened cans which were scaled with slicing force to cause lacerations if someone were to be struck by it.

I suppose these weapons were better than bullets which might be used today.

One thing that always bothered me was the fact that the water which we had to use to extinguish the fires would run down into the apartments of some innocent family below. Naturally this resulted in the destruction of the few items of value which they might own.

Remember that we seem to take for granted that this project was full of people who would participate in these occurrences, but that was not the case. Only a small percentage of hooligans and troublemakers lived here. Most residents of this public housing project were victims of circumstance and lived here, not by choice. They lived here since apartments in other relatively trouble-free areas of the city weren't readily available. Many of these occupants were victims of an emergency need for housing and had to take what was available for them.

Some of the problem teenagers came from other areas and joined the criminal element of Columbia Point for a night of 'fun' and mayhem. By no means were all of these groups teen aged. Adults were almost equally responsible for the unrest.

❧❧❧

This housing project seemed doomed almost from the beginning. When I was in junior high school, most students from Columbia Point attended the William E. Russell School on Columbia Road. I became friendly with many of them and for years I hung around Columbia Point with my friends from school.

It seemed to take a few years, but many of the honest and earnest people saved a few bucks and moved away. They either sought refuge in different public housing in other areas of the city or might have been able to come up with the down payment to purchase a home of their own.

When hard working people left Columbia Point it opened up apartments for others who had little or nothing. This brought in problems such as robberies, break-ins, drug use and other criminal activities.

The neighborhood worsened and was soon ignored by the city. By the 1980s there were only 300 families still living in Columbia Point.

In 1984 an idea was brought to reality when the city turned over the project to the development firm of Corcoran, Mullins, and Jennison who would redevelop the doomed housing into an unusual urban overhaul. Many of the buildings were razed and many others rehabilitated into buildings of mixed incomes. New town house buildings were constructed and the area entertained a rebirth. No more Columbia Point, the neighborhood is today known as Harbor Point. It is home to families of low, moderate and high incomes. It was fully completed by 1990 and received international acclaim for its planning and revitalization.

꙰꙰꙰

It was an exceptionally cold night in January. Ladder 20 had just returned from the third run of the night to Columbia Point. Good old Columbia Point with the most inept elevators in the country kept us busy.

We responded at least daily and sometimes two or three times a day down there. Rubbish fires, stalled elevators, abandoned automobile fires, stalled elevators, apartment fires, stalled elevators, medicals, stalled elevators. You name it, we did it!

People who wanted their cars to never be seen again could drop them off in this area and, presto, instant auto arson.

Not a firefighter of the company needed to look at a building number when they responded. We went down Mount Vernon Street from Columbia Circle to the first left to lower Monticello Avenue or Montpelier Road. Take the second left to Brandon Avenue or Belvoir Road. All the way down Mount Vernon Street to the end for the highrises on Monticello Avenue. These were our least problematic buildings since they were almost entirely occupied by the senior citizen population of Columbia Point.

In one of these high rise buildings on Monticello Avenue lived an older woman named Ethel. Ethel was an invalid and due to her inability to get out of bed she became severely obese. Every few weeks Ethel would fall out of her bed and end up on the floor. Guess who was summoned to return her to the sanctuary of her bed? You are right, Ladder 20 would be called and we would assist her back into her bed in her time of need.

Sometimes I think she was just lonely and her 'fall' may have been self-inflicted. She loved to see us arrive to assist in her predicament.

Columbia Point project could probably have an entire book written about the antics which took place here.

One day Ladder 20 was the designated sandwich run truck. As we were returning to the firehouse with the entire sandwich order we were summoned to an alarm of fire at "Sin City', as everyone knew the project.

We responded to 33 Montpelier Rd. for a report of someone trapped in a stalled elevator. Since we were already on the road we arrived a short while before Engine 43. You see, for several years now no fire company was dispatched alone into the project due to the numerous and all too frequent instances of harassment and the launching of projectiles aimed at the firefighters.

I was the tillerman this day and I had somehow been designated as the protector of sandwiches. By this I mean I was carrying them with me in the tiller seat. Normally the pump operator of the engine was, quite naturally left outside and he doubled as the security guard for the apparatus and all of its belongings. (Including sandwiches).

Since they had not arrived yet we had no protection and our sandwiches were the victims of vandals and thieves. When I returned to my safe haven of the tiller cab, I immediately realized that we were victimized. We performed a search of the immediate area, but nothing was found. Now I wouldn't have minded half as much if the little urchins stole them and ate them, but we were pretty much determined that our lunch was probably thrown into the bay or otherwise destroyed.

❧❧❧

Since we responded to this 40 acre tract of ghetto daily we became fairly well trained and even more capable of performing well at our building fires in this housing project.

After the first line was put into action and charged by the pump operator the ladder company would proceed ahead of the engine guys into the apartment and do a quick search and ventilate as needed. If the apartment was occupied, very often some occupants may still be in the apartment perhaps barricaded behind a closed bedroom or bathroom door. Often times the ladder crew would protect these occupants in place until the engine company knocked down the fire and then these individuals would be removed to the relative safety of the outside.

These apartment fires were just about always one line fires. There just wasn't room for another hoseline in the apartment, but you can bet that the second due engine had a line stretched and perhaps charged in the public hallway just in case.

While the fires received no attention in the media they were a common occurrence and were always extremely hot and produced a maximum amount of steam. Remember that these buildings were constructed of brick faced concrete walls and concrete ceilings and floors. They were, in essence, large ovens where the flammable products inside were usually reduced to embers.

Each living unit had two sprinklers, one in the kitchen area and one in the hallway before most of the bedrooms. The typical layout consisted of a walk-in living room which brought you to into a short hall which usually had a bedroom right opposite the living room. The kitchen was on the other side of the living room wall opposite the entrance door. As you continued down this short hall, you found the bathroom and then came to two or three more bedrooms.

Very often the heat was so intense that the plaster burned off of the walls and ceilings. The bare cinder block construction would be visible after the heat destroyed the living areas. Extension was rare, but occasionally the fire extended to upper floors by the windows in what is known as auto exposure. More simply put, the fire rolled out of the windows and extended upward spreading the fire by convective heat.

⋙⋘

Another common response to Columbia Point was for rubbish in the cellar wells.

When this project was constructed in the 1950s (it opened in 1954) every building had an incinerator. This incinerator was a shaft that ran from the cellar up through a brick chimney exiting above the roof line. On every floor there was a small hatch door where the occupants deposited their rubbish. The rubbish fell down the shaft into a barrel in the basement. When the barrel was full the janitor lit the rubbish on fire and incinerated the trash.

After the burning rubbish barrels were extinguished or just plain burned out, the janitor would remove the barrel and replace it with another empty barrel. The whole cycle would renew itself. Oftentimes the residents would light the rubbish in the shaft on fire because the trash had piled up beyond the first floor. This usually resulted in a smoky hallway and hence someone would call the fire department.

Occasionally the trash would block the shaft above the fire and the smoke would pour out into the hallways on numerous floors. Responding companies would report a clogged incinerator and the firefight was made even simpler than extinguishment. We would arm ourselves with a couple of bricks, go above the clog and simply drop the bricks down the incinerator shaft and clear the blockage.

On Ladder 20 we even carried our own bricks so that we wouldn't have to rely on finding any when we arrived.

With the advent of plastic bags another common occurrence was that when the fire was lit in the incinerator the convective heat might carry a bag up to the spark arrestor covering the chimney above the roof line. The resulting blockage would bank the smoke down throughout the floors and the hallways would become smoke filled.

The companies would arrive, we would traipse up to the roof and climb up to the chimney to free the blockage.

You know, sometimes I think we were highly paid maintenance men.

On rubbish collection day, the janitor would remove the barrels of ash by rolling the barrels on a two-wheeler up the cellar well to await trash pickup at the curb. The cellar well was a sloped ramp with stairs in the center. This enabled the janitor to remove the barrels with no need to lift them.

Sometime in the 1980s the EPA and other acronym government agencies decided that the air quality was being decimated by incinerators such as these and other causes of air pollution. The hatch doors were welded closed and the incinerators became an obsolete area of each building.

The cellar wells became a rubbish collection area when the dumpsters replaced the incinerators. The walk to the dumpsters was a little too much for some of the residents. It became much easier to open the window and pitch the rubbish toward the cellar well. As the rubbish collected in the well the temptation to light it on fire was a fascination imparted on the youth of the area.

I guess it was enjoyable to watch the flames, smell the rubbish burning and await the arrival of the 'firemans' coming in on their fire trucks to extinguish the fire. Little did they know that we slowed down our actions when we arrived and let the rubbish burn longer so that there was little chance of us returning again later for another round of cellar well firefighting that night.

One thing we had to prevent was the extension of the fire to the wooden windows of the first floor apartment when the amount of rubbish was high enough to endanger the occupants of the first floor. It was bad enough that they had to worry about intruders climbing in through their windows and robbing them without worrying about fire, too.

Another thing that always fascinated us was the fact that once we opened the hoseline and hit the fire, the rats came running out of the cellar well. You never stood at the top of the ramp, but played the line over the fence surrounding the well since the rats scampered over each other as they raced up the ramp and pursued their freedom from the water. I guess they didn't mind the fire, but they hated the water.

No overhauling these fires, just drown the crap out of it. Did I ever tell you how much I hated the rats? Not just the rats, but the cockroaches as well.

Captain Dave Watkins in his office at age 78

DFC Vincent A. Bolger as Acting Deputy Chief

FF Rick Connelly Jr., Hingham, MA FD

Deputy Fire Chief George Thompson

Ladder 7's 1976 Seagrave

Ladder 20 and Engine 43

50 Peterborough St. - 4 alarms, 8 dead. (3-31-71)

Vendome after collapse

One of my last fires

CHAPTER 20

I Burned Da Okra!

One of my favorite tales from Columbia Point deserves its own chapter.

One warm summer evening we responded to a struck box for a fire located in one of the seven story buildings on Monticello Avenue at Columbia Point project overlooking the water. The incident was for a fire on the 6th floor. Everyone on Ladder 20 and one member of Engine 43 with the hauling line climbed up to the sixth floor. One cardinal rule that every firefighter respected was that you never used an elevator in Columbia Point!

Upon our arrival at the fire floor we smelled the unmistakable odor of burnt food on the stove. Our lieutenant decided that the best method of gaining entry into the apartment was by aerial ladder and entry from the exterior.

Paul, who was driving, and I went downstairs and we repositioned the truck to the rear below the reported fire apartment. As Paul threw the aerial to the sixth floor window sill, I prepared for the climb. As I approached the kitchen window which was already partially open, I noticed a female sitting at the kitchen table with her head in the bowl in front of her. Before I made entry I hollered loud and clear, "Fire Department! Hey, Ma'am! It's the Fire Department and I'm coming through the window!"

I would never want to be halfway in the window and have someone decide that I was a burglar climbing in the sixth floor window and attempt to attack me. I hollered again so as not to startle the woman and I did not want her to think that I was an intruder. I raised the window sash all the way and made entry into the kitchen. She did not move at all. As I lifted her head by the hair I thought that she was dead. In short time I realized that she had quite a gash on her forehead. She received it when she fell asleep at the table and her head crashed into the bowl. She smashed the bowl and received a rather deep laceration on her head.

By now the pot burning on the stove was giving off some good smoke and the apartment had a smoke condition down to about two feet off of the floor. I was trying to awaken this woman and the crew outside in the public hallway was banging on the door to see if I would unlock it. I turned off the stove and placed the burned pot in the sink.

As she slowly regained consciousness and awakened, I repeatedly told her who I was and when she realized what was happening her cry was, "I burned da okra. Oh, I burned the okra!"

By this time I was crawling out into the depth of the smoke filled apartment, heading for the door to unlock it and allow the rest of the troops in to see the fiasco. As I approached the door on my knees, I caught a glimpse of a person with his arms raised and ready to strike me with something. I covered my head as a reaction not realizing that I had my fire helmet on. I made some type of unintelligible sounds and quickly opened the door and warned my comrades of my impending doom at the hands of a possible assassin behind the door.

As the door swung partially closed and the smoke began to lift from the ventilated windows in the hallway the other guys looked for this armed intruder and promptly let me know what they had found behind the door. It turned out to be a six foot statue. Apparently this statue had been stolen from St. Christopher's Church across from the project and had its face and hands painted black. It was the Blessed Virgin Mary and the weapon she was holding was the infant Jesus.

Strange what the mind can convince you of in the dark with smoke swirling all around you and the 'attacker'.

That was enough to scare me back to church!

CHAPTER 21

The Clements Family and Captain Bob Regan

When I started hanging around at Engine 43 in 1964, I quickly became friendly with firefighter Bob Clements. Bob was the chauffeur of Engine 43 driving Fire Captain Bob Regan.

It turns out that when Bob Regan was a firefighter he drove Fire Captain Bartholomew Clements, Sr. on Engine 43. Now Bart Sr.'s son Bobby drove Captain Bob Regan.

By the way, Bartholomew Clements, Jr was also on the company with his brother Bobby.

A few years after I met Bob Clements he went on to become the aide to District Fire Chief Frank Sikora in District 6.

Chief Sikora was another previous captain of Engine 43.

Confusing? Not really!

〰〰〰

Bob Regan was a major in the U. S. Army Reserve and he was known to many as Major Hoople or Just Plain Bob. Bob was a great guy and he took me for a ride on the apparatus when I stopped in to visit. This was the beginning of a long association with this firehouse.

Bob Regan was also a member of the Ancient and Honorable Artillery Company of Massachusetts. According to Wikipedia, the Ancient and Honorable Artillery Company of Massachusetts is the oldest chartered military organization in North America and the third oldest chartered military organization in the world. While it was originally constituted as a citizen militia serving on active duty in defense of the northern British colonies, it has become, over the centuries primarily an honor guard and a social and ceremonial group in Massachusetts. Today the Company serves as Honor Guard to the Governor of Massachusetts, who is also its Commander in Chief.

Sometime after I had been promoted to Fire Lieutenant, Bob Regan stopped by at Engine 10 for a visit. He was on his way to a meeting of the Ancients as they were known. While he was in the firehouse Engine 10 had a run uptown. I asked him if he wanted to take a ride with us.

Bob had been retired for quite a while now. He was thrilled and could not wait to relate to Kevin Brooks, my chauffeur that day, how the very first time that I had ridden in a fire engine in Boston he was the boss and now today he was riding with me as the boss. So you see how things have a way of coming full circle.

Rest in Peace Captain Bob, Just Plain Bob.

Rest in Peace Bobby Clements.

CHAPTER 22

Captain David F. Watkins, Engine Company 39

Captain Dave Watkins was one of the most memorable and colorful characters in the Boston Fire Department. He was a guy who had been around longer than anyone else I ever knew. I think he was born as the captain of Engine 39.

He was born on February 7, 1894. He was appointed to the Boston Fire Department on October 22, 1920 and assigned to Engine Company 48 in Hyde Park. From there he transferred to Ladder 14 in Brighton. Engine 13 in Roxbury was his next stop.

On July 16, 1937 he was promoted to Fire Lieutenant and was assigned to Engine 1 in South Boston. He later transferred to Engine 15, also in Southie.

At age 61 Dave Watkins was promoted to Fire Captain on April 27, 1955. He was assigned briefly at Ladder 18 before landing at Engine 39 where he was the captain for twenty years. He would ultimately retire from Engine 39. All of his assignments as an officer were in South Boston.

When I was appointed in 1969 Dave Watkins was the captain of Engine 39 and he was on group 3 as well as I would be when I transferred to Ladder 20 in 1971. He was respectfully known as 'Dad' to everyone at Engine 39.

Occasionally I was detailed to Engine 39 and, of course, he would be the officer. It seemed as though every time I was detailed, we would have a multiple alarm fire. There was a church in the South End, a building on Joy Street on Beacon Hill, a serious fire in the MBTA tunnel downtown to name a few.

My last time that I was detailed there to work with Captain Watkins he greeted me at the door as I walked into the firehouse with, "Oh no, it's you. I guess we'll have another fire tonight."

After coming back from the fire of the night the members of Engine 39, including me as the detail guy, were repacking house on the wagon. Captain Dave would assist us by sitting in the old patrol desk area and writing the hose numbers in the hose book.

Every time we would call out a number of the next piece of dry hose that we were repacking the Captain would shout, "What?" The number would be repeated for the benefit of the old gent whose hearing wasn't what it used to be.

The scenario went like this as Fender would shout out, "324Y", the Captain would reply, "What?"

"324Y".

To make it easy on him we would announce, before each piece of hose, "Are you ready?" and of course he would reply, "Go ahead".

"178G"

He naturally would shout, "What?"

"178G" would be repeated.

With the next piece the whole thing played out again.

"Ready?"

"OK"

"821H"

"What?" would come the voice from the patrol desk.

"821H" would be repeated.

After five or six of these Abbott and Costello dialogues, with the next length of hose and the captain's request to repeat the number, Eddie Fender quietly mumbled, "362L, you deaf bastard", to which Dad gruffly replied, "I heard that!"

♪♪♪

Legend has it that one morning when he left the firehouse after a night tour he came across a sailor hitchhiking on Dorchester Avenue. Dave pulled his car over and when the sailor came to the door Dave asked, "Where are you headed sailor?"

The swabby replied, "I'm headed to Quonset in Rhode Island."

Dave said to the sailor, "Hop in. We'll get some breakfast down the street and then I'll drop you off in Quonset."

♪♪♪

At an incident at the old Araban coffee plant in South Boston in-volving a basement flooded with fuel oil the companies were tied up for hours. After a few hours into the standby, Captain Watkins approached the Deputy, 'King George', and announced that he was going to take a little nap in the front seat of Engine 39.

Deputy Chief Thompson said, "OK Cap".

A half hour later 'Dad', all refreshed, approached the Deputy again and told him that he was back.

〜〜〜

I went to a lot of fires with the legendary captain. Not a lot of fires per se, but when I consider how many times I was detailed to Engine 39, I had a better than 80% chance of catching a fire there.

Toward the end of his career another legend, 'King George' Thompson who was the Deputy Fire Chief on group 3, approached Dave Watkins and explained to him that he would be hard pressed to explain to the media how a fire captain who was almost 80 years old was injured or, at worst, killed at a fire. He explained that he thought that Dave should really think about retiring.

After this discussion when Engine 39 would respond to fires, the Deputy would hold them at the ready by his side while putting other companies to work.

〜〜〜

The firehouse where Engine 39 and Ladder 18 were quartered was affectionately known as the 'dump'. It was located at 344 Congress Street in South Boston area where many serious fires had occurred over the years. This area was known as the wool district.

When the tide would come in, it would literally come in the basement of the firehouse.

The fire house opened on May 18, 1891. It was the home to Engine 38 – 39. On February 4, 1947 Engine 38 was deactivated. Engine 39 ran out of there alone until September 26, 1952 when Ladder 8 was temporarily quartered there while a new firehouse was being built in the Financial District of Downtown Boston.

Ladder 8 left Congress Street and headed to their new home at 123 Oliver Street, Downtown on September 11, 1953. Engine 39 was once again a single house.

This turned out to be a short-lived situation since on November 17, 1953 Ladder 18 moved in with Engine 39. This would prove to be a permanent move. Ladder 18 had been quartered three blocks away at 9 Pittsburgh Street, also in the wool district. This firehouse saw occupancy by Water Tower 3, Engine 25, District 5, and District 3 for short periods of time over the years. Ladder 18 had been here since November 7, 1902. This firehouse was razed sometime after Ladder 18 left. It remains as a vacant lot today.

❦❦❦

The firehouse at 344 Congress Street was an architectural masterpiece. The walls were built and then the roof. The third floor was suspended from the roof and the second floor was likewise suspended. The result was a series of rods and turnbuckles which would come down through the firehouse instead of columns. These rods were only about 1 inch in diameter and at night you had to be careful not to walk smack dab into one.

On one of my night details, I was sleeping in a bunk adjacent to one of these rods. Sometime during the night the lights came on and the house gong sounded. The next thing I knew I was on my ass after running into one of these suspending rods.

Today the Boston Fire Museum which is run by the Boston Sparks

Association is quartered in the old firehouse. The fire museum is two blocks away from the Children's Museum on Boston's waterfront.

✦✦✦

Fire Captain David Watkins wasn't still working to make the move on April 22, 1977 to the new firehouse at 272 D Street in South Boston. Shortly before that Dave Watkins retired at 82 years of age and with 56 years of service.

His sack coat hung on the locker door with the following legend embroidered inside on the lining, "I'm good for another 56 years".

There will never be another Fire Captain David F. Watkins or anyone else like him or anyone who will ever serve the City as long as he did.

R. I. P. Davie Watkins, a true legend

CHAPTER **23**

Cheeseburger, Cheeseburger

Across the street from Ladder 20's firehouse was a two street residential neighborhood in the middle of a commercially zoned area.

On the corner of Massachusetts Avenue and Pompeii Street sat a small restaurant named "Mowry's Luncheonette". The Mowry family lived on Pompeii street and had lived there for their entire lives.

This little restaurant did a pretty decent breakfast and lunch business.

In the mid-seventies the Mowrys sold it to a family of Greek immigrants.

Quite often after checking with the officer we would run across the street for a quick lunch to go.

One particular day I darted through the traffic on Mass. Ave. and entered the luncheonette for a cheeseburger and fries.

I ordered from the counterman who turned and with his booming voice hollered to the short order cook behind the window.

"Cheeseburger, side of fries. To go."

As I stood watching the firehouse in case we had a run I heard the burly counterman holler, "Fireman, what's on the cheeseburger?"

Never one for much on my sandwiches , I replied, "Nothing".

Today I actually splurge and get lettuce and pickle, but back then my palate was kinda blah.

As I paid for my lunch and ran back across the street, I headed for the firehouse kitchen and was salivating in anticipation of my haute cuisine lunch of cheeseburger and fries.

As I sat down and unwrapped my burger I was surprised to learn that when you order 'nothing' on your cheeseburger you get...... *a hamburger!*

Be careful of what you ask for!

CHAPTER **24**

You Need a Program to Tell the Characters

Some of the characters in the firehouse were known by names only members of Engine 43 and Ladder 20 may recognize. Some go back as far as Andrew Square, but others were more recent having their origins at 920 Massachusetts Avenue.

There was Daffy Diesel, Buckeye, Timma, Rudy and the Rooster.

Don't forget Cuff's Brother, Baz, Wounded Nee, and Bonzo.

Ally-Pally, Gaylord, Archie, Mucka, And Eddie Big Foot.

If you hung around a while you'd surely have met Jimbo and the Boob.

Other members became known as Woody, Hud, Hughie and the unforgettable Just Plain Bob.

꜡꜡꜡

Firehouse nicknames were not confined to Engine 43 and Ladder 20. Around the city were the likes of Mighty Mouse, Pipe Neck, Hydrant Head, Poopsie, Mush, and Glass Hands.

There was Deck Gun, Hop Up, Powder Balls, Cuffy, Inky, Dingles, and Lo-Lo.

In the South End you would have found Tuck, Shinty, Schultzie, Dirty Plate Nate, Blackie, Balls, the Black Secret, Guppy, the Bull and Crash.

Then we had Tippy, Fender, Big Bird, Hunzie, King George, Towjack, the Major, Sugar, Sarge, Packy and F. I.

In Division Two you may find Gus, The Doctor, Weeds, Bones, Machine Gun, Carlo, Zonka, Humper, Bobo (1637), Pinky, Packy, the Red Rocket and the Lizard.

The reason Bobo has the number 1637 attached goes a long way back. Bo used to tell me that a certain fire officer told him once, "You are only a number!"

From that day forth Bobo had his badge number painted on every work shirt that he owned.

♪♪♪

One guy who knew them all was Joe Toomey. Joe stopped by every morning of the week. He was a bartender at P. J. Connolly's in Andrew Square. All of the years of socializing at 5 Boston Street resulted in friendships that even moving the firehouse couldn't destroy.

Another character who stopped by occasionally was Johnny Georgian. John was the son of a guy who owned a couple of rooming houses on East Broadway just outside of Perkins Square (Dorchester St. & East Broadway) in Southie.

The Georgian House was one of his flop houses and he had a couple more. Most have had fires over the years. One was originally a three-decker and after a pretty significant fire had the top floor removed and was now a two story building.

We used to enjoy kidding Johnny about his girlie magazines. Paul and I would ask him where he hid them so his father wouldn't find them.

He would say in his high pitched voice, "I hide them under the mattress. Who would ever think of looking there? Right? Who would ever look there?"

Yeah John, who would ever think of looking there?

John used to carry around a stack of dog-eared photographs that he had collected over the years. When he took them out to show someone he would say, "This is me and the Commissioner. This one is Joe O'Reilly. You know Joe O'Reilly?"

One of his favorites was one taken from the top of the roller coaster in Paragon Park at Nantasket Beach. John used to narrate this photo with "This one was taken from the top of the roller coaster at Nantasket. My father always says, 'Who would ever think of taking a picture from up there?'

More nicknames, you ask?

There's Moe the Match, Tippy Toes, Tapper, Slippers, Brother Zeke, and La.

Dixie Dan, The Alley Cat, Crazy Horse, Chickie and Johnny Dirt.

You had Hugger, Step Aside, Fuzzy, Fingers, Spanky, Sparky, Spot, the Duke (I've known three of 'em), the Major, Huck, and the Tailgunner.

In the latter half of my career there was Kevin from Heaven, Blob, Five-Heads, Fozzie, Fluffy, Froggy, Broadway Bill, Ben Turpin, and Rocky.

We had the Mighty Midget, Tall Paul, not to be confused with Small Paul.

The late Marty Pierce, Sr. had a nickname for everyone he ever met. Some were complementary, but most were not. If you were listening to one of Marty's conversations your head would be spinning after about five minutes since no real names were ever brought into the fray, just Marty's names.

Rest in Peace, Marty.

CHAPTER 25

Here's Looking at Ya, Kid

About 1000 feet northwest from Ladder 20's firehouse was the City of Boston's Southern Mortuary. This was by no means anyone's favorite place to respond. Fortunately we did not have many occasions to enter this building, but one day stands out in memory.

The lower level of the mortuary had flooded. I don't remember why it flooded, but it did. Engine 43 was summoned to the morgue and asked if they could pump out the cellar area. Arrangements were made and the pump readied to evacuate the nearly four feet of water from the basement.

Engine 43's crew that day was delighted to have one Frank Gambardella working. Frank was known to everyone as Gamby. Gamby could embellish a story like no one I have ever met. If you climbed 14 floors at a fire, Gamby climbed 16, in the dark! Any one telling a story to Gamby probably remembers his reply of, "That's nothing, that's nothing!"

Everyone loved Gamby and we teased him daily since he was about 5' 1". The short jokes knew no end when Gamby was around. He was the last person to know that it was raining.

The firefighters were standing around in the morgue while the water levels were being reduced. Gamby was quite a curious guy and he decided to nose around in this seemly unremarkable building. This was very surprising since he had a fear of the unknown and an even bigger fear of the dark.

There was a cot with a body covered up on it in the hallway. The sheet covered the person's entire body, but there was a plastic bag with numerous organ-looking items on top of the sheet on the gurney. Frankie couldn't control himself and poked his finger into the plastic bag. You should have seen his face when an eye ball came up to the surface. He ran like hell and couldn't stop talking about the eyeball.

Frankie would say, "I stuck my finger in the bag and this blue eye popped up to the top of the bag".

After Gamby's retirement he continued to play softball for the Broadway softball team until he was about 80. Now I don't really remember how old Frankie was when he stopped pitching for the team, but one thing that I do remember was watching his short little legs running to first base whenever he got a hit.

Gamby may have been small in stature, but he was a pretty big guy when it came to his firefighting abilities.

Characters just don't come any better than Gamby.

While we are on morgue stories I remember the night we responded to a struck box for the morgue. They were performing a major rehab and were cutting out some refrigerated units. The cork insulation was smoldering and it took a while to contain the fire.

I was nosing around and opened this large metal door. It had a latch like a walk-in refrigerator. When I opened it to peek inside all I saw were feet and toes with toe tags secured to the big toe.

It was the back door to the units where the bodies were stored awaiting removal from the morgue. It was kinda creepy!

CHAPTER 26

Building Fire on Vinton Street

One cold winter evening we had the usual run to the Columbia Point Housing Project. It was for a stalled elevator on Montpelier Road. Everywhere in the city a ladder truck was dispatched to a report of a stalled elevator with people trapped inside, usually between floors. Due to civil conditions at Columbia Point, an engine company was also dispatched. Today a ladder truck is accompanied by an engine or rescue company to all reports of stalled elevators.

Ladder 20 had just returned from the Sin City run and I was the chauffeur this night. I normally stowed my boots under the chauffeur's seat, however on this run they became dislodged and were sliding out from under. When the 1976 Seagrave ladder truck was backed into quarters, I pulled my gear out from under the seat and was in the process of rearranging it when the box came in.

Box 7236, Dorchester and Vinton Streets for both companies. Both Engine 43 and Ladder 20 turned out quickly since they had both just returned and most of the guys were milling about on the main floor. As they rolled out the door, Fire Alarm is broadcasting on the radio that they were receiving calls for a fire on Vinton Street.

After the 180° turn out of quarters onto Glynn Way and quick right on to Southampton Street it's a straight shot to Preble Street and then a hard left onto Vinton Street. Usually Ladder 20 would go Dorchester Street to Vinton, but I knew that Ladder 18 would be arriving at the same time and we would both be entering Vinton Street from the same direction. I entered from the other end to allow both ladder trucks to gain access to the building.

Just as both ladder trucks pulled up in front of the building, the district chief arrived and notified Fire Alarm that they had fire showing from a three story wood frame building. The fire was in a three-decker with heavy fire exposing the adjacent building on the 'D' side.

I busied myself preparing to drop the jacks and throw the aerial to the roof of the fire building. Ladder 18 was placing their stick on the roof of the exposure building. After raising the aerial I decided that it was a good night for the boots. As I went to get them I realized that they had never been returned to their place under the driver's seat during the commotion with the box being struck. My boots were nice and warm and dry on the main floor of the firehouse. It was a cold night and after two or three hours wearing only work boots in single digit temperatures with plenty of water being tossed around I was pretty damn cold.

During this fire I remember that Engine 10, who responded on the second alarm, was ordered to take a line into the front door. As they crawled down the first floor hallway they didn't see that the floor had burned away and the pipe man, Bill Goglia, fell through the floor and into the cellar. Fortunately he was not seriously injured.

This fire caused heavy damage to the building of origin and also to the exposure building. The second floor apartment of the exposure 'D' building was the home of an off duty firefighter assigned to Engine 17.

Winter time firefighting was always an experience in the northeast. From the first frost until the final thaw it seemed that the city had more fires than any other time of the year.

CHAPTER 27

Three-deckers

If you come from an urban area with closely spaced housing then you are probably familiar with a type of building known as a three-decker. These residential structures are home to three families, one floor above the other.

These are quite literally stacked three family houses. They were built in the late 1880s or early 1900s all over urban area such as Boston, Somerville, Cambridge, New Bedford, Fall River, Chelsea, Framingham, Brockton, Revere and other cities.

Each apartment was similar to the one above with the kitchens being stacked over kitchens, bathrooms stacked over bathrooms and the other living or sleeping areas likewise stacked.

Two common types of three-deckers were abundant. First was the long hallway type where you entered into a long hallway with the living room, dining room, and maybe one bedroom off to the right. To the left were usually a bedroom, bathroom another bedroom and the kitchen. The pantry and the rear stairway were accessible off of the kitchen as was the back bedroom.

The other common style of three-decker was the type where you entered into the living room, passed through the dining room into the kitchen. Off of the kitchen was a short hallway which led to the bathroom and two bedrooms. Once again off of the kitchen were the pantry and the rear stairway with access to the rear porches.

There were variations to either of these depending upon the lot size and depth of the building. One thing in common was that there was never much more than 10 or so feet in between buildings and very often a lot less. Rear yards were tiny and more often than not the rear porches of buildings on the next street over weren't usually much more than 20 feet away.

Most three-deckers had flat roofs resulting in the top floor apartment being extremely hot and uncomfortable in the dog days of summer. A lot of landlords lived on the second floor for many reasons. One was that the heat rose from the first floor and another was the fact that you only had one family above you. You also did not have to climb two flights of stairs with your groceries and your children. This does mean that many landlords didn't live on the first floor.

Each apartment had its own heating system and hot water heater in the basement. You usually encountered a small storage area for each family to keep its clutter in.

Occasionally in some areas of the city you might find three-deckers with a pitched roof resulting in the three and a half story buildings which had extremely high and steeply pitched roofs making ventilation much more difficult than the flat roof three-deckers. These were fairly common in the Mission Hill area and in parts of Jamaica Plain.

Fires in three-deckers were plentiful in the late sixties, the seventies and the early eighties. Most landlords had moved out of the city while retaining their properties as a source of income. They were usually not too interested in the upkeep of their buildings and the tenants didn't worry too much about them either.

Rents were cheap and oftentimes the building was worth more if the owner 'sold it back to the insurance company'. Arson was prevalent in these times. Owners were suspected of arson, but the crime was thought of as difficult to prove.

Three-deckers became vacant and abandoned. Sooner or later they might become victim of the 'unsolvable' crime of arson.

As one drives through neighborhoods in Boston where the remaining three-deckers sit side-by-side you will see many vacant lots. Almost every one of these lots was home to another three-decker which met its fate through arson.

Now I don't mean to say that all of these fires were suspicious or incendiary, but even the accidental fire just contributed to the demise of neighborhoods in Dorchester, Mattapan, Roxbury and parts of Jamaica Plain and Hyde Park.

In the last decade or two new housing has been the trend. The vacant lots have become fewer. New housing has filled in these empty parcels of land and the once prosperous neighborhoods seem to be on the come back again.

CHAPTER 28

Ward Court

One of the worst fires I ever had occurred one November evening just before midnight in South Boston on Ward Court. I remember the day well. It was a Saturday and the daytime saw some four hundred firefighters from Boston take the civil service examination for promotion to fire lieutenant.

Fire Alarm struck Box 724 and announced that they were receiving calls for a building fire on Ward Court. Ladder 20 was first due and when we were traveling through Andrew Square there was a fire ball in the sky ahead.

I was the tillerman this night as I had been for many years prior. Paul was driving and we responded Preble Street to a left on Ward Street and then a right on Ward Court. Ward Court was a small dead end street and everyone would be responding in from the same direction. As we approached Ward Court I was sizing up the area from the tiller seat and did not notice the scene in front of us. The truck stopped at the entrance to Ward Ct. Everyone but me hopped off and ran to the front of the truck. As I started to exit the tiller seat I saw the problem immediately. There was a black female lying in the street in front of us. She would have to be removed before the truck could enter the street and assume its position in front of the fire building.

As we slowly passed the woman I looked down and realized that she was a white woman who was burned around the face and hands and was covered with soot. She apparently was the mother who had been in the house and attempted to save her 4 year old daughter.

Firefighter Peter Nee and I made vain attempts to enter the small two and a half story attached row house. We entered the front door, crawling and were not able to gain access to the living room by the forward door as we entered the hallway. We made another try at advancing down the hallway into the kitchen, but the fire was too intense and the hallway was crowded by tires stored there.

We retreated to the exterior. Peter climbed into the front window which was at ground level. He immediately found a young girl and passed her out the window to me. This was a great attempt at rescue since the house had now pretty much become involved throughout.

After the fire I remember investigating as to why we could not get into the living room from the front hall. The family had placed their living room couch up against the closed door in an attempt to gain some wall space in a fairly small living area.

This whole rescue scenario only took a minute or two. I now had another job to do. When my task was completed on the ground, I returned to my normally primary function which was vertical ventilation.

Paul was on the turntable throwing the aerial to the roof of the adjacent building. Time was a critical factor here if we were to keep this fire from extending down the block through the other 4 or 5 houses attached to the involved one.

I went to the roof and on my way up noticed the extent of the fire. I decided that the best place to vent this particular fire was above the staircase.

This fire was handled with two lines into the front door and one around the rear to prevent extension. Two alarms were struck with a need for manpower to overhaul and check for extension.

This fire was tragic since the baby did not survive and the mother was hospitalized for weeks. The Ward Street area is a tight knit community and the neighbors all pitched in to help the family with clothing, food and a place to stay until the injured mother was released from the hospital and could bury her infant daughter.

The woman's husband suffered burns to his hands after he rescued his seven year old daughter and then attempted to reenter the house to attempt to save 4 year old Pamela. The couple's third child who was 5 years old suffered burns to 30 percent of her little body.

Earlier I stated that this was one of the worst fires I have responded to and worked at. The reason for this statement is that this fire was extremely significant to me since I was a young father with three daughters of my own. I have to tell you that to this day I occasionally have nightmares about this tragedy and how it should have never happened. It is crucial for firefighters to have a few more minutes. A few more minutes to get there sooner and, perhaps, have a better chance to save innocent children like this from a horrible death.

We, as firefighters, continually plead for a quicker detection time, a faster notification time and a response time which is unmarred by traffic, weather or any other obstacles.

᠀᠀᠀

There have been other terrible fires with deaths of children. These are the fires that you carry with you for the remainder of your career and beyond.

On August 7, 1972 there was a horrific fire just after midnight at 6

Gayland Street in Dorchester. Ladder 20 was a second alarm ladder truck. We responded in to the fire fairly quickly since all of the guys were sitting at the patrol desk area listening to the anxious voices of both the Fire Alarm Operators and the company officers.

Three adults and six children were killed at this arson fire set in the front hallway of a large 2 and ½ story wood frame dwelling known as a Victorian. In New York these homes are referred to as a Queen Anne.

Our crew was split up upon arrival. Paul and I found a woman on the third floor and removed her. The rest of Ladder 20's crew found the children. All of them were either in the bed with their mother or huddled under the bed. All dead!

The cause of this terrible tragedy: A jealous husband/boyfriend threw a Molotov cocktail in the front entry way.

♪♪♪

Shortly after this fire Ladder 20 responded up into South Boston to a fire at 38-44 G Street early one morning. When we reported to the chief he ordered us to do a search for four children who were missing. Unfortunately the search turned out in the worst possible scenario. All four kids were found dead.

Fires where children die are the worst part of the job where your best attempts cannot bring about a happy outcome. You feel so unsuccessful and flawed, but what we all know is that time was against us from the outset.

CHAPTER 29

Jumper on the 22nd Floor

In a square block area which was formerly the South Department of the Boston City Hospital there has been a redevelopment and a new complex of buildings was built in the 1970s.

At 35 Northampton Street sits a high rise building formerly called the Nurses' residence. At 860 Harrison Avenue another smaller building formerly called the Doctors' residences. At 755 Massachusetts Avenue is still another building, this one a low rise building which serves as a medical office complex for the Boston Public Health Commission a fitness center, and a retail space on the first floor. In amongst all of these buildings sits a parking garage. Today these two residence type building are privately run and serve as an apartment complex to the masses.

Northampton Tower is a 29 story high rise building containing 246 rental units. The building at 860 Harrison Avenue is a 12 story tower containing 122 units.

Today there is a new plan afoot calling for another high rise tower, this one being 24 stories at the corner of Albany and Northampton Streets.

One warm June afternoon Engine 43 and Ladder 20 were advised by Fire Alarm to respond without sirens to the 35 Northampton St. tower for a report of a jumper.

As we rounded the fire headquarters complex and turned left onto Southampton Street we were able to get a visual on a nurse perched on a windowsill around twenty stories up in what appeared to be a suicide attempt.

It was that time of the year when graduation exercises were scheduled, marks had come out and all the firefighters were thinking, "Oh, God. She didn't pass!"

As we arrived at the main entrance, security knew nothing about why we were on scene. As we explained what the call was about and what we had seen from ground level the question was asked, "What floor?"

No one had anticipated this reception; we all assumed they knew why we were called.

The lieutenant dispatched a member to count the floors and give a report. When the member had counted the floors to the wide open window he also relayed that the nurse was no longer in the window.

Other members were sent to scour the immediate area surrounding the building to investigate whether the nurse had already jumped.

Nothing was found. Security led us up the 22nd floor where they unlocked the apartment door. As we carefully entered the apartment not knowing what lie inside we found nothing, no one.

One member entered the bathroom and pushed the shower curtain aside where we found the 'nurse'. A mannequin dressed in traditional nurse's garb was quietly lying prone in the tub awaiting her rescuers.

No harm was caused by this medical school prank on the day of the release of the grades, but it sure caused some of us to develop a lump in our throats and a knot in our stomachs when we saw 'her' perched on the windowsill.

Pretty funny looking back, not so funny back then.

CHAPTER 30

Snow and Winter

I never particularly liked winter. Winter in the fire service in New England was tough. Cold weather and snow brought out the worst conditions. Hydrants freeze, ladders freeze, hose freezes.

Snowy streets were made even more hazardous when the level surfaces turned into hilly neighborhoods. The ladder truck wasn't going anywhere without tire chains. Today we seem to rely less on tire chains than we did years ago. On-spot chains, the mechanical chains which drop down and spin around under the tire treads are supposed to be an improvement. All-season tires are supposed to be an improvement. Nothing really helps like tire chains, but tire chains leave a lot to be desired today since the apparatus is being built with aluminum bodies.

A company would have two sets of chains (four chains) in the ready when snow was forecast. Most times when the company had a run, your pristine tire chains busted a cross link before you got back to the firehouse. This was especially true when the main streets were bare of snow or ice.

When your company returned to quarters the crew would drop the chains and put on the second set of chains. When this chore was finished, you would then repair the original set by removing the damaged cross links and replacing them with a new cross link. There is a special chain tool which makes this job easier. One side is designed to remove the cross links by spreading open the link attaching the cross link to the main chain. The other side of the tool closes the new link by squeezing it tight onto the main chain. Some nights you could perform this ritual three or four times over. Did I ever mention that I hated snow and ice?

Another fascinating part of the job in the snow was the constant shoveling and salting of the apron in front of the firehouse. After an evening with six or seven runs and the snow starts flying, you can pretty much rest assured that sometime soon the man on patrol will be calling all members down to the main floor to affix the chains and shovel the apron.

The hydrants needed loving too. Each company would be assigned a time to go out and shovel the hydrants in your sub-district. Did I ever mention how much I hate winter?

CHAPTER **31**

The Blizzard of '78

In February of 1978 Boston and the northeast received almost 28 inches of snow. The storm lasted for close to 33 hours. It started snowing and blowing in the early morning hours of February 6th and continued until the nightfall of February 7. The snow fall was made worse by 86 MPH winds with gusts up to 111 MPH. Snow drifts were anywhere from two to six feet high.

One of the guys I worked with called me the night before and said that the weather forecast was calling for extreme snow conditions. He said he thought that we should leave early in the morning and asked if I could pick him up on my way in.

I went outside after talking to him and for the first time in my life I put chains on the tires of my pickup. I left my house around 4:30 am and I picked Buddy up in Weymouth. We then headed for Route 3. After we entered the highway we found that the roads were plowed pretty well. I stopped my truck and we dropped the chains so that we wouldn't burn them up.

I thought that this was an excellent decision until we got into Boston and found that none of the exit ramps had been plowed. We were trapped on what is today known as Interstate 93 with no way off. We passed four ramps that were alternate routes for us, but none were cleared. When we got into Roxbury we found that after all of that concern, the nearest exit ramp to our firehouse was plowed. We exited, but could not turn at the end of the ramp. We had to figure out how to get to the firehouse using detours. It was literally "You can't there from here".

❧❧❧

When the snow finally stopped after 33 hours the city had to begin digging out. The snow piles were so high you just had nowhere to pile the snow. Hydrants were invisible. Sometimes people had a good idea where a hydrant was, but we had to use rakes (pike poles) to stab the snow and wait to hear a clunk.

The City held us over for a 48 hour tour and then let us return home to see our lonely and hungry families for 24 hours. We then came back into work for another 48 hours. It was like doing time. Double shifts in the firehouse and no stores open for days to buy groceries.

The storm left the city virtually immobile. There was a citywide shutdown which kept damn near all of the vehicles off of the roads. Businesses were either shut down completely, or, if open, may not have had electricity. Most ran out of food after a few hours when people found out that they were open.

Buddy and I arrived at 0600 and stayed for two days. Firefighters began arriving extremely early for work, contemplating that travel would be next to impossible. Some of the firefighters walked long distance and others were told to report to the nearest fire station if it was thought that they could not make it to their own firehouse.

Firefighter Ron Richard of Engine 10 lived in Winthrop, just east of East Boston. He made his way to the Sumner Tunnel. Pedestrians are not allowed in the tunnel, but a State Trooper on the East Boston side of the tunnel gave Ron a ride through the tunnel to the downtown Boston side where Ron again continued to Engine 10's quarters on the other side of Beacon Hill.

ﺽﺽﺽﺽ

The streets were impassable for days. Parking on a main street and walking in to fires was commonplace. Ladder companies carried 35' ladders through back yards and up streets to the fire locations. Engine companies carried 250 to 350 feet of line to the only one or maybe two pumps which might be nearest to the fire building.

One eerie thing was to be operating at a fire and not hear the sound of engines pumping and aerials being operated. Only officers had portable radios and those radios were on our fireground frequency and not the main fire channel.

Telephones were used to order multiple alarms which were frequent due to the need of manpower just to get near the fire. When companies did arrive they did so with eight or nine firefighters, but every last one of them was needed to operate.

At one particular fire which Ladder 20 responded to, we were carrying a 35' ladder flat with all of our tools on it. Eight men traipsing through a back yard when we were suddenly stopped by a four foot chain link fence which we ran into. The fence was completely buried and we had no idea that it was there. It must have looked like a circus act with the eight of us trying to climb over a fence which you couldn't even see. After climbing over the fence we proceeded to ladder the fire building like we did at any other fire.

One benefit of the snow piles and drifts was that it made a softer landing for some fire victims who had to jump from windows due to our delayed responses.

During this storm we had a few fires which mandated carrying hose and equipment through backyards and up streets through the 27 or so inches of snow which in some areas had drifted to four feet or more.

The first fire was on Robin Hood Street in Dorchester. This fire was in a 2 ½ story wood-framed dwelling which housed two families. This was the most unusual fire I have ever worked since there were no pumpers or ladder trucks in front of the building. The sounds of apparatus engines, pumps and radios were eerily missing. The officer of Engine 21 was Captain Archie Glover and he had to use the telephone to have the Fire Alarm Office strike a second alarm since portable radios were not very commonplace back then.

♪♪♪

This five day period saw dozens of runs and numerous hours shoveling out hydrants just in case we had another fire. We had some idea of where these hydrants were but we had to use long handled tools to prod the snow banks in order to find out just where they were. Each hydrant took about 15 to 20 minutes to shovel out just to be recognized and to have access to it.

We had one district chief who came into the firehouse and proceeded to berate everyone because he had just come down Dorchester Avenue and didn't see one hydrant shoveled out. After he settled down a bit we questioned where he was looking. His reply was that he was looking out the window as he approached Andrew Square. We had been 'Zonked'.

The lieutenant had to inform him that all of the hydrants on that street were on the other side. He quickly left quarters mumbling something to himself. The Zonk himself had been Zonked!

Another instance found us returning to quarters heading north on Dorchester Avenue. Our radio informed companies that a woman was being brought out of a side street in the bucket of a front end loader about to give birth. The street was only about four blocks from our location. We met the loader and helped the mother-to-be into the cab of the ladder truck and transported her to the Boston City Hospital before junior arrived on the scene.

One of the casualties was a truckload of live chickens heading to the chicken processing plant on D St in Southie. These daily trucks exited the highway and passed by our firehouse. The chickens were headed to their demise at the filthy chicken plant where they would be beheaded and plucked so that you and I could enjoy a chicken dinner. When you passed by the plant the workers would be standing around having a smoke wearing their beautiful white aprons covered in chicken blood.

Well this particular truck overturned while making a turn off of the Massachusetts Avenue off-ramp. The wooden chicken crates broke open and the chickens realized that they had been paroled from their certain fate. Chickens were running around everywhere for days after.

Some of the more enterprising residents decided that they would open up egg farms in their basements or yards. It was entertaining since on numerous runs for next couple of months we would find chickens scattered throughout the neighborhood living in their new masters' homes.

Meanwhile in the firehouse we took in strangers and stragglers. The Red Cross had dropped off cots and blankets in case anyone needed to stay at the firehouse when they were unable to get back home during the storm.

We had citizens that couldn't get home staying at Ladder 20 on Massachusetts Avenue. We had a couple of truckers delivering food-stuffs to the local meat outlets who had to abandon their trucks stay with us. We had a few servicemen who couldn't get back to their ship.

Behind the firehouse was an area known as Newmarket Square. This was the meat district and was occupied by dozens of wholesale meat markets. Truckers would arrive during the night and wait until morn-ing to drop off their loads of beef from the South and Midwest.

One truck was driven by a trucker and his wife. He was low on fuel and didn't think he could run his truck all night for heat. We put him and his wife up for a few days until the market opened again. The trucker asked if it was possible for him and his wife to take a shower since it had been a few days since they had such a luxury. They were accommodated with the use of our large firefighter shower area.

Food had become a problem. Nothing was open for days. No gas stations, restaurants, stores, markets, neither wholesale nor retail. We had nowhere to go to get anything to eat.

One of the truckers broke the seal on his load and we found that we had plenty of beef. We had bread, but butter was a commodity that was lacking. One trucker had a load of wine. Of course the firefight-ers couldn't take a taste since we were working, so we just had to have water. You may believe that or not, but I'll leave you wondering.

A few of our 'guests' were enjoying their free food and lodging so much that after the city was beginning its return to 'normal' we had to evict them.

Eventually the snow left us as it usually does in time. The streets were open again. Parking was once again permitted downtown and in other neighborhoods. Life as we knew it was beginning to return to normal.

ﾉﾉﾉﾉ

After 35 years the Blizzard of '78 is just a memory and some of my readers probably weren't even born yet or were simply too young to remember. My friends, it was fun now that it is a memory, but at the time it was really annoying.

CHAPTER 32

The Drunken Tailgater

All things odd seem to happen as we return from the Columbia Point Project.

On this evening I was the tillerman and it was approaching midnight. As we returned on Old Colony Avenue and then on Preble Street a car driven by a male, the lone occupant, was literally so close that I could not see the front of his car when I looked down over my shoulder.

As the ladder truck approached the red light in Andrew Square I noticed that the driver of the car was so inebriated that he got out of his car and crossed over to one of the neighborhood watering holes in Andrew Square. As he did this he left the car running smack dab in the middle of the street.

Over the intercom, I hollered to Paul, "Don't go anywhere, I am getting out."

Now normally the intercom between the driver and tillerman is always in the receive mode so that the driver hears everything said by the tillerman. If he wishes to speak to me he has to throw a lever over to talk to me.

I assumed that Paul and the officer had heard me. I climbed down out of the tiller seat and leaned in the window of the car. I removed the keys from the ignition and made a quick decision to throw the keys into the rear seat.

As I turned to return to my seat on Ladder 20, I suddenly realized that the truck was halfway through Andrew Square and was heading back to the firehouse minus the tillerman.

You have probably heard stories throughout your life about adrenalin. About how things happen that would never be deemed possible during the normal course of a daily routine.

I literally chased the ladder truck through the square and caught up to it. I reached up to the grab handle and lifted myself up onto the fender and casually climbed back into the tiller seat and returned to quarters with nobody the wiser.

When we backed into quarters and I came down from the tiller seat I asked Paul why he didn't wait for me.

He had no idea what I was talking about and to this day I think he thought that I was just pulling his leg about getting off of the truck in Andrew Square.

The next time I would get out of the tiller seat I would be sure to ring the tiller bell one time. This is the signal to stop.

CHAPTER **33**

I've Got Seven Kids!

One hot summer evening some of us were milling about the rear of the firehouse doing nothing In particular. Suddenly a car heading north on Massachusetts Avenue careened around the corner and headed for the side of the firehouse. The car crossed two lanes of traffic and struck the parked automobile belonging to on-duty Firefighter George Rull.

Everyone ran over to the car and checked to see of the driver was alive. Considering the crash, the noise, and the damage we were surprised to find that not only was he alive, he was not even hurt.

The Boston Police were immediately called and the companies took steps to prevent any other issues from arising out of this accident. (fire, haz-mats, fluids, etc).

When we asked the driver of the car for his paperwork he replied to us that "I don't got a license."

As George stared at the damage to his own car, he was as surprised as any of us to hear this remark.

When we asked him what he meant and why he was driving if he didn't have a license he replied to this question with, "Hey man, I got 7 kids".

Apparently I missed that part of the Massachusetts Driver's License Manual that states that you don't need a license if you have seven kids.

When the Police arrived they towed his car and cited him for various infractions.

The police officer gave George a copy of the culprit's information for George's insurance company and we chuckled when we saw that he lived, where else, but in the Columbia Point project.

Somewhere along the line a friend of his had shown up and was prepared to take this derelict home.

≈≈≈

The story gets better, as they usually do.

About two hours later we get a report of a building fire at 19 Montpelier Road in Columbia Point.

The companies responded down to Montpelier Road along with the balance of the first alarm assignment. As we wound our way through the streets of the project and turned onto Montpelier Road we had fire showing from several windows on the seventh floor of one of the buildings.

As the companies went to work doing what we do best through constant 'training' evolutions at Columbia Point one of the members told everyone else to look at the guy leaning against a parked car outside of the fire building.

Who was it but our old friend with the seven kids grinning like the puke he was. He wanted us to know that he was behind this fire and he was proud to be the one responsible for us having to take our everyday risks for the likes of him and his friends.

Do you know how badly I wanted to take him by the collar and drag him into the fire apartment with us?

Fortunately no one got hurt at this fire. It was a vacant apartment crammed full of every piece of furniture that they could find around the streets of the project. The only real victims here were the occupants of the apartment below the fire who had a fair share of water running down into their homes.

Boy, he really showed us, didn't he?

CHAPTER 34

Wet Hose, Dry Hose

If you are too young to remember repacking hose, let me explain it to you.

When we ran rubber lined, cotton jacketed hose at a fire it had to be rolled if it had been charged. Most of the time if it was run, it was charged. The days of repacking hose in the street didn't start until hose was manufactured using synthetics. If wet hose was repacked it would rot from the moisture, but more importantly sulphorous acid was produced from the water reacting with the rubber jacketed hose.

Years ago it was almost impossible to see a jake without acid holes in his denim jacket and denim jackets were ubiquitous. Many times firemen wore only that denim jacket at a fire.

Hose wagons had a split hose bed meaning that 3 inch hose filled one side and the other side contained 2 ½ inch hose. Usually each half of the hose bed was loaded with 600 feet. When an engine company was ordered to go into a deck gun, the order was usually to lay two lines into a gun.

As I said earlier after this hose was charged it would be rolled and placed on the back step to be transported back to quarters. When you returned, the hose would either be racked or hoisted into the hose tower depending upon which your fire house was equipped with.

Engine 43 had a drying rack which was about 30 feet long so the hose would be placed in this slightly inclined rack with a fold at the higher end of the rack so that the water would drain from the inside and the hose would dry.

Every firehouse had a hose day which in our firehouse was Wednesday. The officer in charge would check to make sure that the hose on the drying rack was dry enough to roll and place on a storage rack. If the hose had only been on the rack for a few days it would probably stay until the next Wednesday.

Another rule in our firehouse was that hose that came back from a fire after midnight would be left for the next day's crew. It would be left on the main floor, rolled just as we brought it back on the rear step of the fire engine.

After returning from the fire, the crews would bring rolled hose from the storage rack to the floor in the rear of the engine company. We had a hose roller which consisted of a round plate connected to a revolving pivot and mounted on legs. You would place a roll of hose on the plate which spun around parallel to the floor and the hose would be fed up to the hose bed and packed by the members.

Each section of hose had a number stamped into the coupling for identification purposes. The last piece of hose in the hose bed would be checked for its number. By checking the hose book and counting back to this number, one would know exactly how many lengths of hose was run at the fire and the appropriate number of lengths would be repacked to assure that 600 feet of hose was in the bed.

Various firehouses had different methods of drying hose. Engine 29, for instance, had a hose tower. The wet hose would be brought to the base of the hose tower. One member would climb the vertical ladder to the peak of the tower. This member's job would be to remove the elevated hose when it was raised to the top by a member whose responsibility was to operate the electric hoist from the base of the hose tower. At the top of the tower were about three dozen wooden pegs which would each hold one length folded in half and hung by the fold.

This method with the electric hoist was a far cry from the horse drawn days when the hose was hoisted by hand. Members at the base of the tower would run the hoisting rope around the fold and hoist the wet hose by hand until it reached the top of the tower where the fireman at the top would slide the fold onto the drying peg , release the hook from the hose and lower the hook back down to the main floor so the whole process could be repeated over and over.

Most old firehouses had a tower and it was a prominent feature of any old photo that you may see.

Engine 17's hose drying rack was in the basement. There is a trap door on the main floor and the wet hose is lowered through the trap door into the basement where firefighters below would take the lowered hose and place it on a rack similar to the rack at Engine 43 which was on the main floor next to Ladder 20 since this firehouse had no basement.

On hose day, members would lower a rake into the hole and the members below would slide the fold over the rake hook and the hose would be brought up to the main floor and rolled and then racked on the hose storage rack.

One other method was a short lived method which never seemed to work well. Some of our one story firehouses such as Engine 22 had large metal hose dryers. Loosely rolled hose would be placed on one of several racks in the 'oven'. The door would be closed and the hose dried inside for a predetermined time. These hose dryers eventually became lockers for storage of equipment or gear. The idea was well intended, but the members never liked the hose drying ovens.

Some nights in the firehouse after the second or third fire, it became absolutely necessary to repack wet hose since there was no more dry hose available.

Ah, the 'good' ole days. Wooden aerials, horses, open cabs and re-packing hose. Another thing of the past from the old days was the all night watch. Oh, wait a minute. We still do that!

CHAPTER **35**

Boston's White Elephant Ladder Truck

You may ask, "Did Boston ever have any fire engines that were not red?" How many of you thought that Boston's apparatus was always red? Well, back in 1941 the city purchased a 1941 American La France 125′ metal aerial with five aerial sections that was painted white.

There are several rumors as to why it was white; all of it is speculation. Some say it was built for Denver, Colorado which had white rigs. Others say it was white to be different. Whatever the reason, Boston bought it and assigned it to Ladder Company 8 in Fort Hill Square. It went into service on September 11, 1941.

This was a new type of apparatus for the city. It had a closed cab, metal aerial, and could operate two ladder pipes at different heights simultaneously. The truck cost $24,000, which was a fairly expensive purchase for conditions in the year 1941.

The narrow streets and parked cars made this piece of apparatus very difficult to drive in the City. All other apparatus had open cabs, except for the 1930 Federals of Rescue Company's 1 and 3. Inside the cab the visibility was bad, looking through the narrow windshields firefighters equated the rig to being inside an army tank. Its overall length was 53 feet, 7 inches, which was 10 feet shorter than the contemporary 85 foot wooden aerial as advertised in the trade journals.

With the aerial fully extended it could operate two ladder pipes, 600 GPM at 125' and 1100 GPM at 65'. It was equipped with a 240 horsepower V-12. It was issued BFD Shop #207. Every piece of apparatus in the city was assigned a shop number. This number was used to track a piece of apparatus from its delivery to its demise.

A short time after this rig entered service the aerial ladder jammed and buckled while on a drill. The aerial was secured with ropes to the adjacent building and eventually cut from the chassis. A representative from the factory in Elmira, NY flew to Boston to supervise its removal. The cost of the repairs was covered under a guarantee from American LaFrance. Rumor has it they tried to re-tract the aerial with the pawls still locked. This was the start of the "jinx."

On November 15, 1942, Ladder Company 8 responded to a five alarm fire at Luongo's Restaurant. 12-16 Maverick Square, East Boston. Ladder Company 8 was assigned second due on the second alarm and took a position on Henry Street. The fire progressed to 3 alarms. At about 0420 hours a wall suddenly collapsed and buried part of the new ladder truck. After the collapse, the 4th, and 5th alarms were sounded. Six firefighters were killed and many injured. Some firefighters blamed the new ladder as the cause of the collapse. They claimed that it was too heavy and its weight against the building brought about the collapse. The building involved was the scene of several previous fires over the years and in all probability the aerial's position had no effect on the collapse. However, this incident served to add to the "jinx" theory. The fire started in a Frio-lator.

One of the firefighters injured at the collapse was Captain John V. Stapleton of Engine 26, who later became Chief of Department, and the father of Fire Commissioner Leo Stapleton. He was on injured leave for almost a year.

This was the first metal aerial in Boston and these firefighters were used to wooden, spring raised aerials. A few believed the wooden aerials would last forever and the metal ones were just a fad that would pass. Somewhere around this time, this rig acquired its nickname, White Elephant.

The deaths, of the six firefighters were quickly overshadowed by the Cocoanut Grove fire two weeks later in which 492 people were killed. Everyone in the area either knew someone or was related to someone who had been killed at the Cocoanut Grove fire. The same group worked both fires.

After the East Boston fire, Ladder 8 needed extensive repairs and it was rebuilt by American La France. It was returned to service as a 100 ft. aerial (one of its five sections was removed) and repainted red. It was in service at Ladder Company 8 from March 2 - June 26, 1944. It was then assigned to Ladder Company 19 in South Boston and their 1930 American LaFrance 85' wooden aerial was assigned to Ladder Company 8.

It should be stressed that many of Boston's firefighters at the time thought that the aerial was jinxed and were actually afraid of it. Some even refused to ride on it. A firefighter who was assigned to Engine Company 2 related that when Ladder Company 19 had the aerial up, some would tell him not to go over the stick, as the building would collapse. Members of Ladder Company 19 were not happy about having the White Elephant assigned to them. The nickname stuck even after it was repainted red.

The apparatus did have some valid problems that may have created some of the myth surrounding its "jinx". The apparatus jackknifed on several occasions and was retrofitted with a trolley brake to better control the tiller section. Brake problems persisted and it was this condition that brought about its end.

On December 3, 1947, while road testing the apparatus with a representative of the brake manufacturer on board, the crew complained about the apparatus "pulling to the left". Ladder Company 19 stopped and Mr. Marivin of the brake company made some adjustments. It was just after they resumed speed, when the truck approached a corner that the accident occurred. The truck overturned along the Strandway in South Boston. Firefighter Joseph Sullivan of Ladder Company 19 was killed.

Just before the end, the brakes may have locked causing the truck to overturn. The chauffeur was Ladderman Joe Babb; Arthur Spacone was the tillerman. Ladderman Spacone was thrown 30 feet, which saved his life. A fund was started for Sullivan's family by Ben Ellis, a well-known fire appliance dealer and Boston Fire Department "spark." Sullivan left a wife and two children.

Cruel fate was not done with Ladderman Spacone. On Christmas Eve, 1959, Arthur Spacone was killed while responded to a false alarm. He fell off the rear step of Engine Company 2. He left a wife and nine children.

This story was reprinted with permission of the author, Firefighter/ Photographer Bill Noonan, BFD, Retired. Appreciation is extended to District Fire Chief John Vahey, retired, for first-hand information regarding this apparatus.

CHAPTER 36

Lieutenant James D. 'Jimbo' Kennedy

This particular character is best described as a gentleman.

One of the firefighters I met on my first night visiting at Engine 43 and Ladder 20 was Lieutenant Jimbo Kennedy. Jim Kennedy was the officer on Ladder 20, group 2 of the old seven group schedule which was worked until December 29, 1969.

In the present day group schedule he was also on group 2 until he was promoted to Fire Captain.

Jimbo had been appointed to the department in 1947 and assigned to Ladder 15 in the Back Bay. He was promoted to Fire Lieutenant in 1954 and transferred to Ladder 18 for a short time. His ultimate goal was Ladder 20 and when he arrived he remained a lieutenant there for twenty years until he was promoted to Fire Captain in 1975.

He returned to Ladder 20 on group 4 as Fire Captain in February of 1976.

﹥﹥﹥

Of all the memories I have of Jim Kennedy I think my favorite was when he would shake your hand and just about crush your hand with his. He would say, "I'm sorry. Here let me shake with my left hand." His left hand was about twice as strong as his right. Ohh, the pain and suffering!

Jimbo was also known as 'Digger O'Dell' since he worked a side job for many years as an attendant for a funeral director.

Ladder 20 was the first company on scene on May 22, 1964 at the infamous Bellflower Street conflagration. As the company was rolling out the door for in-service inspections, the phone was ringing advising both companies to respond to 24 Bellflower Street for a building fire.

As Ladder 20 was responding and crossing over the Southeast Expressway (Rte. I-93) they saw a massive loom up of smoke coming from the vicinity of Bellflower St.

They responded up Boston Street to Bellflower Street and upon arrival the message to Fire Alarm was, "On the orders of Lieutenant Kennedy, strike second alarm box 7251."

This fire ultimately destroyed or damaged 35 multiple family dwellings. Although many firefighters and citizens were injured, no fatalities were recorded.

The fire started on the rear porch of 26 Bellflower Street, located mid-block on a street lined with 'three-deckers' which exist in large numbers throughout Boston. The fire spread quickly to adjoining structures and before long a conflagration was in progress. Dry, southwest winds of twenty miles per hour, and a temperature of 79 degrees helped the fire to quickly advance. At the height of the fire, a large plume of smoke was visible from as far away as 15 miles.

The first notification to the fire department was by a telephone call to the Fire Alarm Office (FAO) reporting a fire at 26 Bellflower Street. A Still Alarm was transmitted at 1338 hours. The FAO transmitted Box 7251 (Dorchester Avenue & Dorset Street) at 1339 hours. The FAO reported to the responding fire companies that it was "receiving calls" for the Bellflower Street location.

After Lieutenant Kennedy ordered the 2nd Alarm District 6 Fire Chief John Greene arrived and ordered the 3rd and 4th alarms. Deputy Fire Chief Frederick Clauss arrived shortly thereafter and ordered the 5th Alarm at 1346 hours. One minute later he radioed "Give me all the help you can get." Acting Chief of Department John Clougherty arrived shortly thereafter and assumed command at Boston & Howell Streets.

A flanking attack plan was devised in order to fight the rapidly advancing fire. This was implemented at the corner of Dorchester Avenue and Howell Street, on the northeast side of the fire. Due to the strong southwest winds, a water curtain was established in order to prevent the advance of the fire in the direction of Andrew Square and South Boston.

Over 250 roof fires were reported during the fire, requiring the response of many fire companies to extinguish. The water supply system withstood the heavy demand for water. At 1530 hours, the fire began to be contained. However, much work was still needed to provide complete extinguishment.

The following buildings were destroyed:

- Bellflower Street: 18, 20, 22, 24, 26, 28, 30, 34, 25, 27, 29
- Dorset Street: 25, 29, 31, 33, 37, 41

The following buildings were damaged:

- Bellflower Street: 17, 14, 16

- Dorset Street: 21, 23
- Howell Street: 22, 24, 26
- Boston Street: 140, 142

❧❧❧

One evening during the softball season in 1977 Jimbo was in attendance at the softball game at M Street Park. He collapsed of a massive heart attack. Fortunately, also attending the game were Larry Holt and Peter 'Frankie' Nee. Both were members of Ladder 20 and subordinates of Captain Jimbo Kennedy.

Larry and Peter performed CPR until relieved by Ladder 19 and EMS. They were responsible for saving the captain's life. For their role in this life saving rescue both were recipients of the Distinguished Service Award in 1978.

In 1986 shortly after the funeral for another member, Eddie Connolly, Jimbo was the victim of another heart attack. This one proved fatal.

❧❧❧

R I P Captain Jimbo Kennedy,
one of the best bosses ever on the BFD.

Thank you to the Boston Fire Historical Society for some of the above information regarding the Bellflower Street fire.

CHAPTER 37

The Hurst Tool

On January 12, 1977 Ladder 20 received one of the first Hurst tools assigned to companies other than Rescue Company 1 and 2. Other ladder companies receiving the tool were Ladders 14, 25 and 27. These tools were assigned to companies in close proximity to roadways with a history of serious motor vehicle accidents.

Those of you who are unfamiliar with the Hurst tool, it is commonly referred to as 'The Jaws of Life'. With it came the usual basic training. There was about 1% of the information available to us then that you will find out there now. There was no internet as we know it. We started the tool every tour. We practiced using the various tips (both of them) and the chains and tried to become familiar with the tool.

One evening we got our first call. Rescue 1's Hurst tool was out of service so Fire Alarm sent Ladder 20 to an MVA on the Mass Turnpike westbound near the Prudential tunnel. When we arrived there was the usual turmoil involved in a three car MVA. Ladder 20's crew was notified that the driver of the gray car was still trapped, unconscious. As we approached the vehicle, I reached inside to check the patient's vitals and made my discovery. The reason the man was trapped had nothing to do with the mangled vehicle he was in, but his seat belt was still fastened under his obese tummy. Needless to say we reminded the rescue guys that we were available to unfasten seat belts any time they needed us.

Our first actual use of the tool came just a few days later. Ladder 20 was notified to respond to Broadway MBTA subway tunnel. A south-bound train had entered the station and a man was in the pit trying to retrieve a fallen item. For some strange reason rather than duck under the platform, the man thought that if he hugged the platform lip maybe the train could squeeze by him. Doesn't work that way! The space between the train and the platform is usually about 1 ½ inches.

When we arrived the man was pinned between the train and the platform at just about his midsection. He was alive and talking to us. Our crew used the Hurst tool to tip the train away from the platform just enough to slide the man out. This may sound easy enough, but remember that subway cars are aluminum so we were concerned about squashing the side of the car and not being able to find a point of support for the tool. We were also concerned about the fact that the man could have fallen about four feet.

Two members of the company grabbed the man by the underarms as Paul and I positioned the tool at a door area. The door area of the sidewall of the car is the area which would be the most reinforced. As we tilted the car, the man was grabbed and cribbing was inserted into the void so that the car didn't release and come back onto the patient. The man was remarkably in good condition with some ripped clothing and a massive priapism.

Following my promotion in1987, members under my command have since used the Hurst tool or the Amkus tool dozens of times, but these incidents reported above were the initial offerings of a tool which is responsible for the saving of many lives.

CHAPTER **38**

Firefighter John T. Aleks

You may occasionally see that I mention Columbia Circle. This is the rotary that connects Day Boulevard, Morrissey Boulevard, Columbia Road and Old Colony Avenue.

Let me make my apologies to Firefighter John Aleks right now. If he was around, he would remind me that it was Kosciuszko Circle not Columbia Circle. The Rotary was named for Tadeusz Kosciuszko. He was a Polish freedom fighter and engineer. Kosciuszko endeared himself to this country during the American Revolution and later gained even greater recognition in defense of his native Poland.

John was an Andrew Square Polski and had no problem reminding us younger guys that there was a certain Polish ancestry alive and well around the Andrew Square neighborhood. Never say Saint Mary's Church to John or you'd quickly find out that it was Our Lady of Czestochowa.

On Boston Street there is the 'Polish Club'. Its proper name is the Polish American Citizens Club of South Boston. Outside the club is a statute of General Casimir Pulaski. Pulaski was a revolutionary War cavalry officer born in Poland and praised for his contributions to the U. S. military in the American Revolution. He is better known as 'The Father of the American Cavalry".

⌁⌁⌁

One thing that always baffled me was why John spelled his name *Aleks* and his brother Joe (the mayor of Andrew Square) spelled his name *Alecks*. Well, in spite of that fluke, John was a great firefighter with the biggest hands I ever saw.

John was like a lion. He was one of the best and toughest firefighters I ever worked with, yet he had the personality of a lamb.

For example, I was washing the ladder truck one morning. As I approached the fifth wheel area I accidentally soaked John who was washing Engine 43. I immediately dropped the hose and ran around to the other side of the truck to apologize for wetting him.

John's reply to my concern was, "Hey, it's only water. If you're afraid of a little water then you're in the wrong business."

I spent the next week or so looking over my shoulder to see when I was going to be a victim of payback. I fully expected revenge from John. It never came.

John had two odd interests. First off I noticed years ago that John always seemed to be cutting wire whenever we had an abandoned auto fire.

When I asked why he did this, his reply was, "I have a 55 gallon drum in my cellar at home. I always cut a piece of wire and strip it. I throw the wire in the barrel. When I retire I am going to take the barrel to the junk yard and cash in my copper wire."

His other odd interest was his 'paper flattening'. I call it flattening since I never saw anyone else ever do this.

John would ask guys to bring their old newspapers into the firehouse and leave them in a pile. He would take the newspapers, open them up flat, and place the individual pages in a stack which he then sold to the flower wholesaler where he worked part time.

I guess they wrapped flower bundles in them. John was paid pennies per pound for the paper. Hey, it kept him quiet.

Rest in Peace, John.

CHAPTER 39

Boston: Automobile Arson Capitol

In the 1970s and 1980s there were more automobiles burned in Boston than in the rest of the Commonwealth combined. People who never wanted their car to see the light of day again would make arrangements with 'someone who knew someone' to make their car go away.

When a car was stolen either professionally or by an amateur who just wanted to use it for a few hours it would rarely be recovered. It was usually found burned. Where else would it be burned but in Roxbury or Dorchester. Occasionally a few cars would burn in East Boston, Charlestown or even downtown by the waterfront.

The same streets saw autos burning nightly, some even more than once. I remember the night we had an automobile burning on Robey Street in Dorchester. An hour or so later we had another car burning directly across the street from the first one. The first car still had steam coming off of it when we arrived for the second one. This section of Robey Street was one block long and there was only one house still standing, but not occupied at this time.

Engine 21 and Ladder 20 used to respond to Box 1734 located at East Cottage and Batchelder Streets. If the box wasn't false it was probably pulled for an auto on Robey Street. Auto arson was so common here that we adjusted our route to 1734. We used to respond in to the box from Marshfield Street to Robey Street to East Cottage Street just so that we could check the cars abandoned on Robey Street.

When I would be stationed at Ladder 7 later on we had our nightly autos burning at the end of Howe Street or at the end of Dewar Street. I have responded to over one thousand auto fires in my career.

Automobile arson just wasn't a priority back then. In the 1980s, at the urging of the insurance industry the rules changed. Before you could collect on your insurance a party would have to go to the Fire Investigation Office at Ladder 20's old firehouse location. You would need to fill out a form and answer some questions asked by an arson investigator.

Things changed and the auto arson problem became negligible.

CHAPTER **40**

Deputy Fire Chief George Thompson

From my first days on group three I realized that the commanding officer, the highest ranking chief in Division One was Deputy Fire Chief George Thompson. 'King George' as he was affectionately known was a command presence. When 'King George' was on the scene, you knew it and respected it.

Now this nickname was not a jab at how he ran a fire, but it was a title due to his size and his command presence. Anyone who has studied leadership knows that a command presence is very important. You are in charge and others must be aware of it. There was no doubt about who was in charge when C-6 was on the scene.

His voice and stature preceded him. He was tall in his white fire coat and white helmet. George was not around to see bunker gear. I do not think he would have liked it, but that is just my opinion.

This man, this leader of men, was way ahead of his time. Young firefighters feared him as I did in my younger years. Some of us chose to bend the rules, but not George Thompson. The work uniform was chambray shirt and dungarees, not tee shirts.

The man on patrol was to be stationed at the patrol desk dressed in a uniform cap and black tie. When a chief officer entered quarters the man on patrol was to rise, salute the chief and announce the last box to be struck and if the all-out was in. The next step would be to announce the chief in quarters via the public address system. When I was appointed to Engine 29 the fire station did not have a P A system and the call bells were still being used. When the call bell system was used there were certain signals designated by a series of rings to announce a chief in quarters, each member was assigned a number, and a long ring meant that everyone was to hit the main floor.

Some chiefs did not care whether this procedure was followed, but you can bet if Deputy Chief Thompson didn't get the last box and salute, then your officer was going to get an earful. When your officer heard about it from the Deputy then you were going to hear about from your officer. Rarely did Deputy Chief Thompson speak to firefighters about a wrongdoing. He followed the rank structure and spoke to your officer and then you knew that the officer would let you know about it.

I specifically remember one day when King George entered Engine 43's quarters to perform his quarterly inspection. Our boss on group 3 was Lieutenant Paul McNiff. I overheard the Deputy telling Lieutenant McNiff that the condition of quarters was acceptable with one exception. He said, "Paul, I hate those T-shirts and don't want to see the men in them again." Naturally the lieutenant called us to the main floor and relayed the deputy's feelings on tee shirts.

Another thorn in George Thompson's side was long hair on firemen which was the style in the 1970s. If he saw a member with hair which was deemed to be inappropriate according to the rules he would positively let the officer know that one of his men didn't comply and needed a haircut.

The rule, at the time, was that the hair wouldn't touch the collar and a mustache would not interfere with the donning of a face piece used with the Self Contained Breathing Apparatus (SCBA). Better to be trimmed than to be seen by the Deputy.

One evening we had a fire on East Broadway in South Boston. Ladder 20 was the second truck company. Arriving companies had fire showing from the third floor and heavy smoke coming off of the roof of a three story wood frame residential building. Paul positioned the truck and I prepared for my climb to the roof. As I was preparing myself for the climb to the roof, I heard District Fire Chief James Murphy order a second alarm on this box. I knew that Deputy Fire Chief George Thompson would now be responding and everyone had better look their best and be doing the right thing.

As I was approaching the roof, people on the fourth floor roof of the exposure D side were hollering that there was an unconsciousness man on the roof. When I reached the roof and stepped off, I opened the penthouse door for ventilation and quickly removed the victim by carrying him down the aerial.

These days in BFD history were prior to the ambulance service and EMS as we know it today. If you needed a transport to the hospital the Boston Police paddy wagon did double time as an ambulance. The medical equipment available was a stretcher in the wagon and the inhalator (O2) that you brought with you. As you bounced around in the back of the patrol wagon with no rear door, you were lucky if you were not a second patient by the time the ambulance reached the Boston City Hospital.

At this time in history the hospital was run by the City of Boston and was known as Boston City Hospital. This was before Boston Medical Center was ever a twinkle in anyone's eye.

As luck would have it we got the patient to the emergency room safe and sound with him regaining consciousness somewhere between

Perkins Square and Andrew Square. I had to wait around while the police officers did their paperwork and then they would transport me back to the fire scene..

As I walked down Broadway to the scene of the fire, I found that the fire was knocked down and the companies were making up. On this night tour we had an acting lieutenant in charge of the company, Eddie Flynn from Engine 33. He met me at the front of the ladder truck and told me that he had a message from the deputy. I was feeling pretty good about my 'rescue' at this point and although the gentleman whom I removed from the roof was certainly not exactly in a life threatening situation I thought that perhaps the deputy left a message for me stating "tell that kid he did a nice job" or something to that effect.

Alas, that was not to be. The message the deputy gave to A/Lieut. Flynn was, "Tell that man to get a haircut".

♪♪♪♪

Deputy Fire Chief George Thompson prescribed to two principles that everyone was aware of. First, if he told you to stand by, you had better be standing right next to him in case he needed you. Secondly, when he gave you an order you had best be where he sent you and nowhere else.

Chief Thompson was way ahead of his time when it came to always having an additional company available in case he needed it. It was always easier and faster to deploy an available company than to decide that you needed another company and had to strike an additional alarm and wait for it.

He also had his people deployed in a fire building and knew where every company was working.

When we were young and restless and always anxious to go to another fire, we thought that Deputy Chief Thompson was a prick and he was a tough boss. It took twenty years and a promotion before I realized that he was probably one of the best, if not the best chief I ever worked for. You were not going to get hurt at a George Thompson fire.

Here's one more story about King George before we move along. Just before 2100 hours one evening I was sitting alone doing my watch. Fire Alarm called C-6 on the radio and asked the chief to call Fire Alarm. Well the chief and his aide must have just been approaching the firehouse because all of a sudden I looked up and there coming in the front door was the Deputy.

I had no tie, no uniform cap and no chambray shirt on. I was dressed in the dreaded tee shirt with our company logo. I hopped to my feet, announced the last box and saluted the man. As I picked up the P A mike to announce him in quarters, he informed me that he was only here to use the telephone.

He must have been on hold because he cupped the phone and asked if this was my watch. I replied that no, it was not and I was just covering the floor for the man on patrol. I couldn't believe it; I had just lied to the deputy. If he had looked in the house journal he would have seen that my name was entered as being on patrol and I would have been screwed.

I don't know why, but I have always felt as though he knew that I was not being truthful, but decided to not make an issue over it. Right then and there I decided that never again would I lie to an officer. I would be a man and take my lumps if I was wrong. How's that for some startling advice, 'Man up Sonny'.

ﾉﾉﾉﾚ

Well, Deputy Chief Thompson had a glorious career in the BFD and went on to retirement. I secretly realized that we might never see the likes of George Thompson again and the BFD would be the worse for that.

Many years later I would be assigned to Engine 10 as a Fire Lieutenant. We were stationed with the Deputy of Division One at 123 Oliver St., downtown in the financial district. Word reached us that Deputy Fire Chief George Thompson had passed away. Another legend in the Boston Fire Department had gone to the big firehouse in the sky. Apparently he had been residing out-of-state and word did not reach us until after he had been already buried. No one would be able to pay their last respects to one of the greatest fire chiefs to wear the uniform of the Boston Fire Department.

A quick word on retirement; it always is a fear of retirees that they may enter a firehouse and not be recognized by anyone. Shortly after the 10-15 was struck for Deputy Fire Chief George Thompson, Division One, retired another retired district fire chief came walking into the firehouse. It was warm and the overhead doors were up, but I recognized the man heading toward the patrol desk.

As he neared me I said, "Hi, Chief". Instantly his face beamed as he was recognized. He said, "You know who I am?"

I replied "You are Chief Ed Campbell from District 8".

Well his day was made. Unfortunately I had to inform him that George Thompson was already buried.

We passed a few words back and forth and then he left. I think that he must have been saying, "Boy, that guy is old if he remembers me".

❧❧❧

The District Chief for years in East Boston, District 1, was Angelo Corolla. Angelo wasn't too fond of having Deputy Chief Thompson come into one of his fires and takeover. Let's just say that they didn't see eye to eye.

One evening Chief Corolla had a box in for a block of stores on Meridian Street, just outside of Central Square. He reported that he was investigating upon his arrival. The chief's next report was that he had a fire in a block of stores.

The following report was that he had three lines run and all companies were working. Deputy Chief Thompson decided to take a ride to East Boston and see what was going on.

In years gone by units had to report that they were on the other side of the tunnel since radio reception in the tunnels was impossible. You had to let Fire Alarm know that you had been out of contact for the last few minutes in case they were looking for you for an alarm.

As Deputy Thompson arrived in East Boston he advised Fire Alarm that "C-6 is on the East Boston side", Upon hearing this Chief Corolla knew that the jig was up and ordered a second alarm quickly followed by a third alarm.

I guess King George's feelings were correct on what was going on in District 1 at this escapade on Meridian Street this evening.

❧❧❧

In District 6 in South Boston, District Chief Jim Murphy was another one who didn't want King George snooping around at his fires. He figured that if he said nothing on the radio when he had a fire then the Deputy would leave him alone.

Murphy's aide was a fellow named William 'Bud' Newman. Early on Bud had told us that when he reported "Car 6 is on the portable", that meant that they had something. Back in those days only chiefs and company officers had portable radios.

Many nights we would be responding up into Southie to a struck box. Car 6 would call off at the location. A minute or so later Bud would tell Fire Alarm that Car 6 would be on the portable. To Engine 43 and Ladder 20 responding from the other end of the district the message was the same as saying, "Pull your boots up, we're going to work!"

Man we had some good fires in those days.

R. I. P. Jimmie 'Deck Gun' Murphy.

♪♪♪

After Deputy Fire Chief George Thompson's retirement he was approached by Leo Hughes of Rescue 1, who was the President of the Boston Sparks Association, to come to one of the club meetings and be the guest speaker.

Surprisingly the chief agreed to come and speak. Before the meeting he admitted to all in attendance that he had never done this sort of thing before. Nobody would have ever known if he hadn't told us because he was one of the best speakers with some of the most interesting stories that the club has ever had.

I think that the most interesting story that he told was of a fire on Washington Street, downtown. The fire was in a store and the deputy was concerned about extension into the clothing store on the 'D' side.

Chief Thompson ordered a ladder company to investigate the exposure building for extension. A short time later the red- faced officer returned to the Deputy and told him that the cop would not let them into the clothing store to investigate.

Chief Thompson immediately summoned the police sergeant over and asked why this cop was acting inappropriately. The sergeant said he would investigate and get back to the deputy.

When the sergeant asked the rookie police officer why he wouldn't let the firemen in, he replied, "You told me not to let anyone into the building ".

The sergeant angrily replied, "I didn't mean the firemen, you idiot".

R. I. P. Deputy, you were way ahead of your time!

CHAPTER **41**

Marine Unit Not Needed

Directly across the street from Ladder 20 was a series of streets which were not exactly world class thoroughfares. Each one ran for only one block and took you deeper into an area of mercantile and factory type buildings.

As you came up Massachusetts Avenue there was Island Street, Chesterton Street, Pompeii Street, Peirson Street, and Rusfield Street.

The only two of these streets with residential properties were Chesterton and Pompeii Streets.

After 6 pm the sidewalks were rolled up in this neighborhood and there was nothing to do, nowhere to shop, and the local kids depended upon the firehouse to access the candy, soda and cigarette vending machines.

We knew all of the neighborhood kids and most of their families. A lot of the families were related.

We hardly ever responded to either of these two streets on business throughout the sixties, seventies and into the eighties.

One night we received a still alarm from Fire Alarm to respond to some kind of fire on Island Street. It was around midnight and traffic was light on Massachusetts Avenue which was a one way street against us.

As we exited the firehouse we saw a fairly good size glow coming from behind the diner at the intersection of Mass. Ave and Island Street. Paul decided to buck the traffic, what little there was, and headed the wrong way on Mass. Ave then turned left onto Island Street where we found the source of the glow.

We had a fully involved boat sitting in the middle of Island Street burning from stem to stern. Not just a rowboat or a dinghy, but an 18 footer.

The report to Fire Alarm was that "We are on Island Street with a boat fully involved and you can cancel the Marine Unit if they are responding."

Comedians all around us!

CHAPTER 42

But Santa Does It Every Year

Unusual happenings seem to be a way of life to firefighters. Take the young adult male who thought he could burglarize the drug store on Devine Way in South Boston by climbing down the chimney. This individual must have thought that since Santa Claus arrived via the chimney that he could enter the drug store in the same fashion.

I can only imagine why a person would have a desire to burglarize a drug store. I suppose it has to do with drugs and therefore you need to understand that a person is probably not thinking too clearly in the first place.

The problem arose when he realized that there was no fireplace, but that the chimney only led to the oil burner in the basement.

Somehow people heard his screams for help in the middle of the night and the fire department was summoned by the police for a ladder to investigate the noises coming from the roof of the block of stores on Devine Way in South Boston. When Ladder 20 arrived they discovered that the screams for help were coming from the chimney and things were placed in motion to rescue the idiot Santa from his plight.

Since this predicament happened before the days of technical rescue teams, this guy was brought to the roof by lowering a rope fashioned into a loop down the chimney so that it could be drawn around his shoulders and under his arms. He was hoisted by a number of fire-fighters into the waiting arms of the Boston Police Department.

Charges: breaking and entering in the nighttime while an idiot.

Lieutenant Paul Lentini and FF Jimmy Gibbons

On the afternoon of January 6, 1981 a serious fire occurred in the building located at 16 – 17 Arlington Street in the Back Bay.

During this fire a portion of the upper floors collapsed trapping Lieutenant Paul Lentini and Firefighter Jim Gibbons along with four other members. These firefighters were trapped for hours while members of the department worked to free them. As the rescue attempts were being undertaken the fire continued to burn on the floors above the trapped members.

A surviving firefighter was trapped for hours on top of one of the deceased members. He was traumatized for so long that it affected his return to duty.

8 alarms were transmitted to knock down the fire and rescue the injured firefighters. The recovery process continued for hours while the rescue and recovery team struggled to ensure that no more members were either injured or killed.

The box transmitted for the fire was 1539 located at Arlington and Newbury Streets. The first alarm for the fire was at 1508 hours and the eighth alarm was at 1553 hours. The 8th alarm was struck after the collapse and Deputy Fire Chief Gerald P. Hart also ordered Rescue 2 and Ladder 30 to the fire.

Fire Lieutenant Paul M. Lentini, age 32, of Engine 37 with ten years of service and Firefighter James M. Gibbons, age 31, of Engine 37 with six years of service were both killed in the Line of Duty.

⚶⚶⚶

I was working on this day which started off as a fairly busy day tour. There was a two alarm fire in Dorchester. Ladder 20 left the firehouse to cover at Ladder 23's quarters during this fire.

As we proceeded up Magazine Street headed to Blue Hill Avenue we came across another building fire on Magazine Street. Lieutenant Dick Salerno ordered the box struck and we went to work at a fire in a two and a half story wood frame residential occupancy.

When the fire was knocked down we were ordered by the Fire Alarm Office to continue on to Ladder 23 for our cover. Shortly after our arrival at Grove Hall the first alarm was struck for the fire at Arlington Street.

If Ladder 20 had been in our own quarters we would have eventually arrived at the fire, however since we were covering at Ladder 23 we responded as Ladder 23 on Box 1539. Our afternoon eventually saw us covering at Ladder 15 on Boylston Street in the Back Bay.

⚶⚶⚶

On the night tour of January 7, 1981 we again reported for work. It was an average night tour with numerous runs, but nothing of significance until later in the night when Box 5358 located at Commonwealth and Chestnut Hill Avenues was transmitted.

This fire eventually went to nine alarms. The fire was in a block long five story residential apartment building. The fire consumed most of the top floor.

Ladder 20 started on our way to cover at Ladder 22 in Oak Square, Brighton. Only minutes after our arrival at Ladder 22 Fire Alarm ordered us to respond to the fire.

This was the same group working at this fire which 18 hours ago had just lost two members in another multiple alarm fire that saw most of the same companies working. Fortunately nothing out of the ordinary occurred at this fire.

R.I.P. Brothers Paul Lentini and Jimmie Gibbons

CHAPTER 44

Layoffs, Company Closings and Kevin White

1981 saw the vindictive and cold political ploys of one of the worst mayors the fire department has ever had to deal with. Between White (1968 – 1984) and Tom Menino (1994-2014) we have never been held as anything but a thorn in the mayor's side. Ray Flynn was between the two (1984 – 1993) and he didn't treat us much better.

The unusual approach that Mayor Menino took was that, even though he hated the fire department, we received some of our best contracts under his regime. Who knew?

Even with a brother on the Boston Fire Department, Mayor Ray Flynn stiffed us after a six year wait when he suddenly left the city to become the Ambassador to the Vatican. Our union took three zeroes in the six year contract that was negotiated after he abandoned us. Good waiters get good tips was the phrase that became famous under Mayor Flynn. (And a Southie guy at that)

While White was in office Proposition 2 ½ was passed in the legislature. Under Proposition 2½, a municipality is subject to two property tax limits:

1. **Limited taxation:** The total annual property tax revenue raised by a municipality shall not exceed 2.5% of the assessed value of all taxable property contained in it.
2. **Tax increase limits:** The annual increase of property tax cannot exceed 2.5%, plus the amount attributable to taxes that are from new real property.

A side effect of Proposition 2½ is that municipality income will decline in real terms whenever inflation rises above 2.5%. Historically inflation has been above 2.5% for a significant majority of the years since 1980 (22 out of the 28 years to date), thus resulting in a real decline in local tax rates and local spending ability.

An exception allows the citizens of each municipality to override the 2½ restriction to address specific needs of the community thus giving the citizens direct control over their taxation.

The tax coffers were drying up in City Hall and White needed more money to run the city. What better way to make his case than to use the dedicated city workers such as cops, public works employees, teachers, and firefighters as tools for his gain.

With the passing of Prop 2 ½ the City was pitted against the state, the teachers were pitted against the police, fire and public works employees. The mayor was pitted against the City Council and the Boston delegation in the state house. Mayor Kevin H. White was pitted against Governor Ed King, where there was never any love lost anyway.

Boston was mired in severe financial problems. Firefighters and cops were being laid off and the schools almost closed. White went to the state house with a bailout program nicknamed the Tregor Bill. It was named after Norman Tregor who sued the city over unfair taxation.

As I previously stated White used public employees as pawns in his political game. He laid off firefighters and cops and then hired their replacements on overtime because he knew that the numbers of personnel available to work were impossible to deal with.

White directed the fire department to close companies and cause a public clamor over neighborhoods being under protected. White assumed that by frightening the public with the reduction in fire companies and fewer cops on the streets the legislators would be pummeled by calls from their constituents demanding a return to safe numbers.

The fire department was decimated by the closing of fire companies and ultimately a reduction in on-duty firefighters, layoffs, demotions and a general destruction of the morale of the fire department.

February 4, 1981

On February 4, 1981 the following companies were disbanded: Engine 25, Engine 43, and Ladder 20. This was the closing of my beloved firehouse and one Engine Company in the downtown financial district.

This would only be the start. As each group of companies saw their closing, hundreds of firefighters were laid off. These layoffs were heartless. Minorities were protected and this action only served to exacerbate racial tensions.

April 10, 1981

On April 10, 1981 the following companies were closed for good.

Engine 1 in South Boston

Engine 12 in Roxbury

Engine 26 in the South End

Engine 34 in Brighton

Engine 40 in East Boston

Engine 45 in Roslindale

Engine 54 on Long Island

Ladder 5 in West Roxbury

Ladder 8 in the financial district (which was quartered with Engine 25, already closed) This closing left only Rescue 1 and the Deputy of Division One in the firehouse.

Ladder 22 in Brighton

Ladder 30 in Roxbury

Ladder 31 on Long Island

Aerial Tower 1 in the South End

Engine 50 in Charlestown was closed but the firehouse was taken hostage by a citizen's group and the outcry of the neighborhood resulted in the firehouse being reopened on May 9, 1981. The City didn't expect the residents to be so vociferous and demanding. Who dare question City Hall?

The firefighters who were laid off were strained in their relationships. Families collapsed, houses were lost. The City didn't care. The only solution would be the passing of the Tregor Bill we were told over and over.

October 20, 1981

More layoffs were coming and more company closings.

October 20, 1981 saw the shuttering of Engine11 in East Boston, Engine 36 in Charlestown, and Ladder 13 in the South End.

Engine 11 was quartered with Engine 5 and District 1. This company was also taken hostage by the community, but it was never reopened.

January 14, 1982

The final straw was on January 14, 1982 when Engine 49 in the Readville neighborhood of Hyde Park was closed along with Rescue 2 in Roxbury, and Aerial Tower 2 in the Neponset section of Dorchester.

Engine 49 was also reopened after much demand from the neighborhood on July 21, 1982.

To show his commitment to this nonsense, Mayor White's neighborhood firehouse was boarded up when Engine 10 was moved from Beacon Hill to the downtown fire station with Rescue 1 and Division1. They were relocated to this firehouse which had already seen Engine 25 and Ladder 8 disbanded, but Engine 10 was sent there to be quartered forever. Another ladder truck was to be reestablished at this firehouse on May 21, 1983 when the Tower Company was introduced.

On February 3, 1984 a much needed fire company was put into service on Long Island to relieve the companies from Dorchester from making daily treks out to Long Island. Engine 54 and Ladder 31 had been stationed out there and a skeleton company now referred to as the Fire Brigade was established.

So the tale of politics was played out for the masses to adjust their lives to. Many firefighters to this day have not forgotten and never will for one reason or another.

♪♪♪

Up until the day of Kevin H. White's funeral on February 1, 2012 I was completely unaware that he had become St. Kevin. On the day of his burial the local television stations preempted regular broadcasting. The politicos strutted to his wake and his funeral and praised all of the good that he had done. Not one of the many people interviewed seemed to remember the Tregor Bill and the mayhem bestowed upon the firefighters, police officers and teachers during the Proposition 2½ fiasco.

Maybe some of the laid off cops and firefighters might have given a more emotional eulogy; one that might have opened some blind eyes.

Kevin, See ya!

Section Four
Ladder 7

CHAPTER **45**

Welcome to Ladder 7

As I arrived at Ladder 7 and met the few individuals that I didn't know very well, it didn't take too long to realize that I now was working at a very busy company, even busier than Ladder 20 had been.

On my second day tour, a Sunday, the first run of the morning took us to Rosseter Street on Mt. Bowdoin. Upon our arrival there was smoke showing from a 2½ story wood frame house on the corner of Bullard Street. Ladder 23 took the front of the building. Ladder 7 came up Bullard Street to the 'D' side of the house and established our position.

Tom McGovern was driving and threw the aerial to the roof. I was riding the side and was assigned as the 'Open up man'. My job was forcible entry and, along with Lieutenant Brad Rattigan, made entry into the side or rear door. This entrance opened up into a small hallway which led to the kitchen.

As we opened the door we were met with a fairly intense smoke and heat condition. We dropped to our knees where we still had a slight amount of visibility, crawled into the kitchen and almost immediately found an adult female victim lying on the kitchen floor unconscious. We removed her to the exterior where she was treated by Boston

EMS. Rattigan and I returned to the same area where we had found her.

In a hallway off of the kitchen we ran into Ladder 23's crew and my lieutenant and I entered one of two bedrooms with Ladder 23 taking the other. Between both companies we found two more victims, both children.

Sadly, all three members of the same family succumbed to the severe smoke which made it impossible for them to escape. The fire itself was not unusually devastating and was knocked down by the engine companies in short fashion.

District Chief Bolger struck a second alarm to get more help there as he was well aware that both of his first alarm trucks were engaged in search and rescue.

Well, this was only my third tour here and already I've had a multiple casualty fire. I was to find out that this was quite the norm. Daytime or nighttime, weekday or weekend, accidental or intentional, fires occurred in this neighborhood almost daily.

❧❧❧

Late one evening while Ladder 7 was returning from a run down around Commercial Point, we were given a run by radio for an infant not breathing on Dickens Street.

Since we were not responding from quarters, our route brought us into Dickens Street from the opposite end. As I approached the address I saw a woman standing on the front stoop cradling an infant in her arms.

I stopped the ladder truck with my driver's door even with the front door of the house. I set the Maxi brake, hopped out and the woman, as panic stricken as she was, quite literally threw the infant at me, from her arms to mine.

I glanced at the months old baby and saw no sign of life. My EMT training kicked in immediately. I cradled the baby in the crook of my left arm, listening and feeling for signs of breathing. I began infant CPR with two fingers on the baby's delicate chest. I entered the house, sat on the sofa, and continued working the baby. Inside I was dying. I was praying to hear a gasp or a sob. I heard nothing.

One thing I remember like it was yesterday was that when the ambulance crew arrived, they took a look and saw how comfortable I was and threw me with the baby into the back of ambulance and transported everyone to the Carney Hospital in Dorchester.

We arrived at the ER and that was the last I saw of the little girl. Unfortunately, as happens so many times, I had to ask around for the outcome and was finally told that she didn't make it.

Upon my return to the firehouse I called my house and demanded that my wife check on my son. She thought I was a crazy man, but eventually understood how these things affect us sometimes.

Ⳏ Ⳏ Ⳏ

One hot summer evening a couple of kids ran up Parish Street to the firehouse screaming, "They're killing him! They're killing him!"

After getting them to calm down enough so that we could get the story we responded down to Downer Court. In the street was the victim of a severe beating. Whatever this kid did to someone was enough to cause him to receive a beating by baseball bat.

The teenager's face and head was so contorted that identification was probably difficult at best.

How could someone hate someone else so badly that this could happen? I have asked myself that question over and over.

Drug overdoses, heart attacks, shootings, stabbings, victims struck by motor vehicles, electrocutions, and falls. Any of these scenarios are enough to warrant a response by the fire department, the police and EMS.

Dorchester saw a lot of deaths and injuries on a daily schedule. Other parts of the city did their share as well, but our response district kept us busy.

These scenes described above are the causes of the accidental victims being injured or killed. There are also a number of injuries or deaths which are caused by the distraught individuals hell bent on dying of their own choice.

I have to tell you that the suicides bothered me so much because of the senselessness of the deaths. As I heard many years ago, "Suicide is a permanent solution to a temporary problem".

CHAPTER 46

Meeting House Hill

As the closing of Ladder 20 appeared imminent the members were asked to put in a paper requesting three choices of companies for reassignment. My paper requested Engine 21, Ladder 7 or Engine 18. Paul's first request was for Engine 21.

Deputy Chief Ed Kenney called one day when we were working and asked if we wanted to make a choice. The Chief said that Paul was going to Engine 21 and asked which of my other two choices I wanted. I said that I would really like Engine 21 also, but he told me that there was only one opening and Paul had got it. I really thought long and hard about going to Engine 18, but realized that I loved truck work so I chose Ladder 7.

When the terrible day arrived and the firehouse was closing, I asked some of the guys who were using a fire department pickup truck to move equipment if they would mind dropping off my locker at Ladder 7's house. There would be three of us from Ladder 20 going to Ladder 7. Pat MacAuley, Artie Johnson and I were staying together up the street.

Al Marshall would be going to Engine 17 in the same house as us.

I not only got my second choice, but was able to stay on group 3 and work with the guys that I knew from working at fires together. Two of the other group 3 firefighters were classmates of mine from the Fire Academy. Tom McGovern, Jack Brignoli and I would be together with Bob White and Lieutenant Brad Rattigan on Ladder Seven, group three.

Coincidentally there were three other members of our drill class on Engine 17. Paul Spacco, Jim Pyke, and Frank Shaughnessey were joined by the three on the truck and now six of the sixty FFOPs from the December 24, 1969 class were all in the same house.

Ladder 7 and Ladder 23 were contenders for the busiest truck each year. Sometimes Ladder 23 padded their runs and beat us out for busiest. Sometimes it was Ladder 7. One thing about being busy is that you miss a lot of other runs which would push up your statistics, but there are only so many hours in a tour.

If I thought that I went to a lot of fires on Ladder 20 then I found my-self going to even more fires while on Ladder 7.

Ladder 20 was doing about 4300 runs per year, but Ladder 7 was doing right around 5000. It was an extremely busy period during the history of the Boston Fire Department.

Remember that we had the arson ring of the 80s that I mentioned in Chapter three making sure that we didn't sit still for long.

Some of the fires attributed to this arson ring were the following

- St. Philips Church, 889 Harrison Avenue, Roxbury (abandoned)
- Laredo Street, Roxbury (vacant apartment building)
- St. Johns School, 50 Dacia Street (abandoned school)
- 318 – 322 Adams Street, Dorchester (multi-unit apartment building)
- 844 – 848 Dorchester Avenue, Dorchester (vacant three deckers)

- 410 E Street, South Boston (toy factory)
- 165 Brookside Avenue, Jamaica Plain (vacant commercial building)
- 386 Washington Street, Dorchester (vacant YMCA)
- 97 – 99 Sydney Street, Dorchester (vacant three deckers)
- 356 Centre St., Jamaica Plain (3 ½ story wood commercial building)
- 2401 Washington Street, Roxbury (vacant 6 story former hotel)
- 20, 22, 24, 30 Bromfield Street, Downtown (4 story commercial)
- 7 Montgomery Street, South End (vacant Clarendon Street Baptist Church)
- 19 Bartlett Square, Jamaica Plain (vacant cellophane factory)
- 99 West Fourth Street, South Boston (4 story commercial building containing the Boston Sparks Association)
- 296 Freeport Street, Dorchester (Minuteman Tire Company)

These were some of the major fires set by the arson ring. Not included were all of the smaller, less spectacular fires set on a nightly basis.

Many firefighters suffered injuries and many more residents were burned out of their dwellings in these fires set by a ruthless group of individuals for a less than reasonable justification of creating more public safety jobs. Unbelievable as it is one Boston Police officer and one Boston Firefighter were involved.

❧❧❧

One night around midnight we received a call from Fire Alarm to respond to Box 3148, Dorchester Avenue and Adams Street. We responded from quarters, left on Adams Street to Dorchester Avenue. There was nobody around and nothing showing. Fire Alarm was notified that both companies were returning to quarters from a false alarm.

Almost immediately Fire Alarm struck box 1895, East and Winter

Streets for a building on Fifield Street. As we responded back up toward the firehouse less than a mile we had a three decker fully involved. Boy those guys were good at what they did!

The false alarm was a deterrent to get us away from the neighborhood while they did their thing.

♪ ♪ ♪

I spent about 4 years on group 3 and then we ended up with a new captain after the retirement of Fire Captain Warren A. Hardy. Captain Hardy was another unforgettable character and a firefighter extraordinaire. He had a career where he had served on busy companies all of his life and finished up that career on Ladder 7.

Our new Captain was Paul J. Greene. Captain Greene came to us from Engine 20. He will never admit it, but I think it was too slow there for him. Captain Greene asked me if I wanted to come over to his group (Group 2) and be his chauffeur. I told him that I would consider it a pleasure. I joined my old friend Mark Callahan on group 2 and remained on group 2 for the rest of my stay on Ladder 7.

While working with Paul Greene I met his son Jimmy. Jim used to come up to the firehouse and hang around with his dad. Later on Jimmy was hired by the Hull Fire Department. Like most sons of firefighters he wanted to someday be a Boston Firefighter. He moved to Boston, and took the civil service exam and was lucky enough to be called for a job.

I met Jimmy again when he was going through the Massachusetts Fire Academy after being hired by the Town of Hull. I worked there as an instructor in the Recruit Firefighting Program.

Shortly after he was hired in Boston our paths crossed again. Jim was assigned to Ladder 29 in Dorchester. He wasn't there too long when he was promoted to Fire Lieutenant and again we met when he was assigned to Engine 4 as a lieutenant. I was recently promoted to captain I was temporarily filling in as the captain of Ladder 24.

Jim Greene was relentless in his studying just as his dad had been. It wasn't long before he took the captains' exam and he did extremely well. He was quickly promoted to captain and was assigned to a few places including Engine 33 in the Back Bay.

More studying brought another promotion to Jimmy's career. He is now a district chief and don't be surprised if some day in the near future you see his name in orders when he is promoted to deputy chief. Jim is now assigned to District 4 in the South End/Back Bay.

❧❧❧

I enjoyed my years on group 2 with Captain Paul Greene and we continued going to fires as Ladder 7 always does. After I was promoted a few of the guys asked if I was coming back to Meeting House Hill, but in my heart I knew that I never would. I am not a believer in returning to a firehouse where you were assigned as a firefighter. You are now a boss and have to enforce rules that you probably stretched or even broke when you were a firefighter.

Over the years when an officer is forced to discipline a member I have heard guys mention the following phrase, "Boy, does he forget where he came from."

It is not a matter of where anybody came from. You are an officer now and are expected to perform a different job than you did as a firefighter. You are now responsible for the conduct and the discipline of the members under your command. My thoughts on the subject are, "If you wanted to be one of the 'good ole boys', then you should have refused the promotion when it was offered to you."

Busy, busy times at Ladder 7!

CHAPTER 47

Firefighter Jack Brignoli

The Boston Fire Department strikes special signals over the tappers, bells and radio for various reasons. Special Signal 10-15 is struck after the BFD is notified of the death of an active or retired firefighter. The striking of this signal signifies that the National Standard (U. S. flag) be lowered to half-staff until the day of the funeral. This system is a great tradition so that the members are aware of the passing of retired members and it demonstrates that we have not forgotten.

Usually the entire BFD is aware of the passing of an active member long before the striking of the 10-15.

As I write this chapter 10-15 is struck and Jack Brignoli's death is announced. Jack was 76. He was a classmate of mine from December 24, 1969. We would end up working together for six years at Ladder 7.

Jack was a controversial character who had no qualms at all about expressing his opinion. Jack had varied interests, but his most treasured was his family. His garden was right up there with a passion for the betterment of the Boston Fire Department.

You might meet people who would tell you what a troublemaker Jack Brignoli was. Upon further investigation they had never met nor worked with him. For years Jack tried to convert the Mutual Relief Association funds into a better plan. His concern was so that there would be more money available to help out destitute members and the families of deceased firefighters.

This passion of his followed his reputation for years. Jack knew that the funds could be better invested and his attempts at reorganization of the Mutual Relief Fund met a brick wall at every step of the way.

Jack was a building wrecker before, and after, he was appointed to the BFD. His knowledge of taking a building apart was surpassed by none. He was solely responsible for the introduction of the adze into the fire service. Now anyone familiar with construction and destruction of buildings knows that the main instrument or tool involved is the adze. Jack felt that the ax, Halligan, pike pole or rake and other tools known to the fire service could be greatly enhanced by the introduction of the adze into the BFD's arsenal of tools.

Jack would spend hours instructing new firefighters, members of Ladder 7 and anyone else who had an interest in doing the job more efficiently and easily in the techniques involved in mastering the use of the adze.

Today you would be hard pressed to find a ladder company without an adze.

Like many firefighters, I was not originally interested in change. Firefighters are the worst ever when it comes to change. We have tools that work well and why do we need to change them?

Members of the BFD would still have horse drawn apparatus if they could. They would still be wearing chambray shirts and dungarees and would wear dungaree jackets and work boots at fires if someone didn't make them change.

Transition to the lime yellow color of fire apparatus was an example of the members insisting on holding their ground. This new color was not a good idea and it was proven that it 'sucked' over and over. That's why most fire engines are red today as they always have been. Red is the fire service, blue is the police.

I learned from Jack and we certainly had our differences, but we both were man enough to realize that no one agrees on everything. There was one night tour that Jack and I had a real brouhaha. We were nose to nose and each had our fingers in the other's face.

We left for home the next morning and reported for work again the day after. I arrived before Jack and was sitting in the patrol desk when Jack arrived with his usual flair. He approached me and the first thing that he said to me was, "I suppose you and I will be like the other guy. We'll never speak again".

I looked at Jack and told him in no uncertain terms that the other night was the other night and this is a new day. I said, "It's over, Jack. We both had something to get off of our chests and it's forgotten".

In amazement, Jack looked at me and said "Really? No hard feelings?"

"Jack, we are both men and we are not going to ruin our friendship over one little disagreement, are we?"

Jack never disagreed with me after that. We had discussions, of course, but nothing serious. Jack worked for years with another fire-fighter and the two of them never spoke. As unbelievable as it seems, two hard heads, Jack and Tom, that just couldn't stick out their hands and say "Let's get over it".

※ ※ ※ ※

One thing that we both ended up agreeing on was the acceptance of the adze. It was proven that it was the tool for overhauling, forcible entry and general destruction work in finding hot spots, ventilating and removing stubborn items that were in our way.

You can open a roof with it, remove baseboards and trim, break windows, and quite naturally force entry into any locked door with the adze. Any tool has a purpose and limitations. It must be used properly. Let the tool do its job and do not try to 'bull' your way through.

One famous tale in the annals of Jack Brignoli history was the Black Mountain episode. A teen age autistic boy became lost on Black Mountain in northern New Hampshire. He had been camping with his family and had wandered off on his own. Jack has a son who is also autistic.

After hearing on the news one night about the plight of the teenager, Jack got in his car and headed for Jackson, New Hampshire and Black Mountain. He drove for four hours headed for a location he knew nothing about. Jack was not a camper, but he knew in his heart and mind that he could find this boy.

Jack had never hiked before. He started up one side of Black Mountain and came down the other with no luck. He made a start up another area and while headed to the summit again, he heard the sounds that he recognized from his own autistic son. He located the boy and got assistance to help in retrieving the teen and removing him to the safety of his extremely worried and distraught family.

Now Jack would have told you that he was by no means a religious man. He and I had many discussions about religion and God. Jack knew that he would, not could, find him.

⟡⟡⟡

Rest in Peace, Jack. You've earned it.

CHAPTER 48

Firefighter Edward R. 'Eddie' Connolly

During my first few years on the job Massachusetts Bay Community College offered courses off campus at the Boston Fire Department. These classes were held on week nights at fire headquarters. I decided that this would be an interesting endeavor since I felt that anything that I could do to increase my knowledge and education concerning my job would be beneficial to me in the future.

I began to attend some courses at headquarters. My first course was "Introduction to Fire Protection". My instructor was Joe O'Keefe. Joe was a well-spoken gentleman who made the topic interesting and entertaining.

Joe was from Salem, Massachusetts and would later become the State Fire Marshal.

I followed this course with 'Water Supply' and then another course, the title of which escapes me right now. The water supply course was taught by a District Chief from Boston, Walter Maraghy.

It was while attending these courses that I met Eddie Connolly. It turns out that Eddie was on Ladder 20. I was still on Engine 29, but would shortly become a member of Ladder 20.

Eddie and I hit it off pretty well. When I was transferred to Ladder 20 I actually worked with him on group 1 for a short while until I was reassigned to group 3, where I stayed for the duration of my time on Ladder 20.

Eddie was tall and lanky and had a fantastic sense of humor.

We had some great times together and he taught me some facts about the job which I have retained throughout my career. One of many tips that he bestowed upon me was how to force entry into a house through a window doing as little damage as possible.

You take your axe and lay it on the windowsill horizontally placing the blade under the lower sash. Now by using a prying motion you snap the tongue off of the sash lock and, bingo, you are in.

I taught this forcible entry method for years while an instructor at the Mass. Fire Academy. Every recruit who graduated between 1996 and 2006 received the "Eddie Connolly' through the window quick entry tip.

>>>>

Ed and I played cribbage both on and off duty. We continued to be cribbage partners for years. We even spent lunchtimes together when one of us would be off duty and would stop in for our daily cribbage games. If I remember correctly the final tally of our years long crib-bage tournament was Eddie: 348 and me: 43.

Eddie was one of those guys whose face was constantly formed into a smile. He loved a good practical joke and was pretty damn good at pulling one off.

Life became kind of strange when Eddie bought a house in Pembroke, MA and shortly after I bought a house about one mile from him in

Hanson, MA. During this period he put in a pool. After I saw his pool, I said, "Hey, you did all of the legwork, I guess I'll use the same pool guy". I put the same type pool in, too.

A few years later I moved to Quincy and shortly after Eddie moved about six blocks from me in Quincy, also.

When Ladder 20 was closed in 1981, Ed transferred to Ladder 17 in the South End when I went to Ladder 7. We didn't see each other at work too often anymore since he was on group 4 and I was on group 3.

After a short time on Ladder 17 he was asked by District Chief Arthur 'Archie' Glover to become his aide. And so it became Aide to the Chief Eddie Connolly driving DFC Archie Glover.

᚜᚜᚜

On March 21, 1986 there was a nine alarm fire in South Boston on Mercer Street off of Dorchester Street. The fire was in a three decker with exposure fire damaging the two buildings on either side of the main fire building. It has been my observation over the years that wood frame buildings rarely collapse and when they do it is under extreme conditions. The front wall of this building pulled apart from the other walls and collapsed into the street.

Sitting in front of this house was a tree which is a fairly common sight in Southie. The tree sat on the sidewalk a foot or so back from the street. This tree was dead and, for years, the neighborhood had been trying to get the city to remove this unsightly thing from their street.

When the front wall pulled away from the main structure it hit the dead tree, knocking it over into the street in front of the fire building. As it fell it struck the tiller cab of Ladder 18 and then landed on three firefighters out front injuring two and killing the third, Eddie Connolly.

Eddie was another good friend whose funeral I attended. The number of funerals a firefighter attends in his career is staggering. Eddie Connolly left behind his wife, Pauline and a son, Jimmy and a daughter, Barbara,

Today Barbara is a senior Fire Alarm Operator which is the equivalent to a Fire Lieutenant. Jim Connolly, just in the past month or so, has retired from occupational injuries which he has received in the line of duty at his assignment at Ladder 6.

A few months after Eddie's funeral the square at the corner of Columbus Avenue and Isabella Street in the South End was dedicated to the memory of Firefighter Edward R. Connolly.

We gathered one Sunday morning outside of Ladder 17's house preparing for the dedication. His wife Pauline was supposed to pull a rope which would drop the black bunting which had been draped over the memorial plaque in anticipation of the unveiling.

When it came time for Pauline to pull the rope, it was stuck and would not release the bunting. Immediately I knew that Eddie the prankster was up there holding the whole thing up so that he would have the last laugh on all of us.

The square is directly outside of District 4, Engine 7 and Ladder 17's firehouse.

Firefighter (Aide to District 4) Edward R. Connolly was a Line of Duty Death on March 21, 1986.

RIP, my good friend you are still missed daily.

CHAPTER 49

District Fire Chief Vincent A. Bolger

One of the greatest chiefs that I have ever worked with was Vinnie Bolger, my district chief when I was on Ladder 7. Chief Bolger believed in always having enough help on scene to do the job safely and efficiently.

I was fortunate enough to have him choose me as his aide during the last year of his career. Chief Bolger wore out aides at a fast pace. His original aide was Eddie Homer whom he brought with him from the days when Vinnie was the captain of Ladder 12. When Eddie retired he was replaced with Kenny Rogers. Kenny was followed by Willie Austin and then me.

Chief Bolger was a well-liked chief who had the interests of his men foremost in his thoughts. I mentioned earlier in another chapter that some chiefs waited until all of the companies were on the scene before returning anyone. Chief Bolger was one of those chiefs. This bothered some members who might work off group and occasionally you heard gripes about Vinnie Bolger. You never heard any bitching from the firefighters on group three. His firefighters loved him and they loved working for him. Vin Bolger was the only chief that I ever worked with who called me at home after I was injured at one of his fires.

He was the most level headed and unexcitable guy I have ever run into on the job except maybe for Deputy Chief John 'Chickie' Kilroy.

❧❧❧

I remember one night in particular we were responding to a box alarm in Fields Corner. The box was 3182, Adams and Park Street. We were responding from Grove Hall, the home of Engine 24 and Ladder 23.

Neither 24 nor 23 went to this box and the first due companies were from our firehouse on Meeting House Hill. As we approached the general area, Ladder 7 called off with 'heavy fire showing'. I took a quick look over at the chief and saw nothing, no reaction. Ladder 7 quickly returned to the radio and ordered a second and third alarm. Once again I stole a glance at the chief and saw nothing, no reaction.

I was ready to jump out of the car and he didn't even blink. He had no reaction at all. Later when I asked him how he remained so calm when we were not even at the fire yet for which three alarms were ordered, he replied, "What was I going to do, we weren't there yet."

As we approached the fire, coming down Adams Street there was, quite naturally, a glow in the sky to match exactly what we had. It was a six family three story wood frame duplex, fully involved. The arson ring was at it again tonight and they had done their usual great job doing what they did.

After I ditched the district car out of the way, my first move was to circle the building checking for exposures in the rear. I surveyed the area, checking for access to the building, hydrant locations and anything else of importance which I might need to report to the chief.

As I returned to the front, the 'A' side of the fire building, the Chief said, "Where were you, I was looking for you".

I told him where I was and gave him a quick update on conditions in the rear and on both sides.

He replied "Fine, now strike a fourth alarm and when you get done doing that, strike a fifth."

Chief Bolger was 'old school'. He never used the radio, that was his aide's job. He trusted your opinion and he used your eyes as his second set.

This blaze was one of the most spectacular fires that I had ever worked. We used enough water on this large six-family house to float Noah's Ark down Adams Street.

༄ ༄ ༄

In December of 1971, fire was pouring out of the eight-story Dorchester apartment building located at 677 Dudley Street at the corner of Alexander Street when District Chief Vincent A. Bolger first arrived.

Dozens of panicked residents who did not speak English were hanging from the windows and balconies of the overcrowded building, a rundown hotel formerly known as the Gladstone near Uphams Corner.

Using a smattering of Spanish that he had taught himself, Chief Bolger shouted, "No salte! No salte!" to urge the victims not to jump.

Chief Bolger oversaw the rescue of more than 125 men, women, and children via aerial ladders that night. The blaze left more than 450 people homeless. One man, who was deaf and mute, died.

"Hub fireman's Spanish helps avert disaster" read the Boston Globe front page headline the next day. The episode helped spur the city to teach basic Spanish to firefighters, according to news reports of the period.

"He was a legend in his time and still is," said Robert Winston, a retired Boston Fire District Chief who was a young fire buff in the 1960s when he first met Chief Bolger.

"He was an absolute gentleman. He knew the job very well and conducted himself in a most professional manner no matter where you saw him. He was very different and likable and was really revered by everybody on the job who knew him," said Winston, who lives outside Atlanta.

Bob Winston himself went on to become a district chief. I believe that he modeled himself after Chief Bolger in his career as a district chief. Bob retired and went to become the fire chief in a few cities southwest and south of Boston.

〉〉〉〉

Chief Vinnie Bolger, a longtime resident of Dorchester, became a Boston firefighter in April, 1943, he was promoted to lieutenant shortly after and was a lieutenant on Ladder 4.

His next promotion took him to the rank of captain in 1955. While captain he was assigned to Ladder 12 and Ladder 30. Bolger was promoted again, this time to district chief in 1967.

As a District Chief he was assigned to District 7, which includes Dorchester and a portion of Roxbury, from 1970 until his retirement in 1981. Chief Bolger spent 38 years in Boston's fire service.

"He was like nobody else. He was way ahead of his time," said Mike King, a retired Boston Fire arson investigator. "He left the rank in the car and he'd come over and talk to you like a friend," King said.

Chief Bolger was remembered for his impeccably clean, pressed uniforms and his friendly manner with firefighters.

On calls that turned out to be false alarms, Chief Bolger would stay on the scene and wait for the engine companies to arrive. He would wave at the firefighters as a sign of respect, or take a few minutes to chat.

"At a fire, he was a total professional and he was always watching out for the life and safety of the firefighters," Winston said.

Born Vincent Augustine Bolger Jr. on Feb. 2, 1917, he was a Navy veteran who enlisted a few days after the attack on Pearl Harbor in 1941.

When the deadliest nightclub fire in US history broke out at the Cocoanut Grove in Boston on Nov. 28, 1942, the Navy dispatched him to help with a makeshift morgue. Some of the 492 fire victims were sailors or Marines.

Chief Bolger was also known for his deep respect for New York City firefighters.

"He always looked up to those guys from New York," King recalled. "He had a way of wearing a New York helmet to aggravate people."

He also was one of the founding members of the Boston Sparks Association, a club started in 1938 for fire buffs. The association has grown to over 200 members and now runs the Boston Fire Museum in South Boston.

ﹱﹱﹱ

Another fire I had with Chief Bolger was early one Saturday day tour. It was his first tour back from vacation. He and his wife, Pauline, enjoyed themselves on a week-long cruise. He was pumped and ready to get to work.

At the time the fire department administration was trying different methods to reduce responses and have enough companies available for another fire.

This experiment was the use of the 'A' companies. While fire alarm would strike a box for a report of a building fire, only the first two engine companies and the first ladder company would respond initially. The third engine and the second ladder truck were marked with an 'A' and would only respond if multiple telephone calls were received or if the first arriving companies reported smoke or fire showing or if they requested the 'A' companies.

Fire Alarm struck box 1765, Howard Ave and Sargent Streets. Engine 17 and Ladder 7 were the 'A' companies for this box so only District 7 responded initially. The fire location was on Sargent Street. Engine 21 turned into Sargent St. just ahead of us and Lieutenant Riley ordered Fire Alarm to start the 'A' companies.

The fire building was a 2 ½ story duplex with smoke showing on the right or 'D' side. Now upon his arrival Lieutenant Riley saw the smoke but apparently did not feel a report of smoke showing was warranted since it was light smoke and appeared to not be too serious. Ed Riley was an extremely experienced fire officer who had spent his entire career in very busy companies.

Engine 21 ran their line around to the rear to the source of the smoke and Engine 24 ran a backup line into the front door of this vacant structure. Ladder 23 threw their aerial to the roof and initiated the process of ventilation. Overhaul operations were saved for the arrival of Ladder 7. Engine 17 ran a dry line to the front of the fire building.

The fire was in the rear kitchen area of the right side of the duplex. When I reported this to the Chief he asked if we had done anything while he was on vacation.

I told him that things were pretty dead while he was gone and I hoped that he had brought some work back with him.

That was when he told me to "Give them a working fire and let's get things rolling again".

The working fire order started an extra engine and Rescue 2. The Deputy also came to all working fires. When Deputy Chief Jim Finn arrived and walked up the street his first words to Chief Bolger were, "I knew you were back, it's been too quiet."

♪♪♪♪

One of the better parts of driving the chief was our daily visits to Grove Hall, the quarters of Engine 24 and Ladder 23. All three firehouses in District Seven were quite busy places. If you wanted to catch a fire any of these firehouses were the place to be.

Chief Bolger and I ate supper at Grove Hall nightly. The same men who would work their asses off for Vinnie Bolger also cooked for us each night.

Jay Donahue, Mike Gover, Steve Langone, Dan Polvere, Captain Jack Force, Lieutenant Bob Dorsey, Dave Hale to name a few. You don't find better firefighters than these guys.

It was not uncommon for these companies to have three or four fires a night, while two was probably more the norm.

Chief Bolger knew what he could expect from these firefighters and he protected them well. He appreciated what they were capable of.

♪♪♪♪

One day tour we had a fire right at the start of the tour. It was cold out, everyone wanted to put this one out and get back to the warm firehouse. After the fire I was in the shower when another run came in for District 7. I quickly dried off and jumped into dry clothes, slid the pole and got into the car. The chief looked at me and asked what I had been doing. I replied that it was 'shower time' and I apologized for being slow to come down. His answer was that he wasn't worried about my being late, but he didn't want me to get out of the car all wet like I was and catch pneumonia.

♪♪♪

I remember one night when Ladder 20 was still in service. Fire Alarm struck box 1881, Hancock and Trull Streets for a fire on Rill Street. Engine 43 and Ladder 20 did not respond to this box on the first alarm. Engine 21 called off with 'Fire showing'. Naturally everyone in the firehouse gathered around the patrol desk since both companies would respond to the 'working fire' or second alarm if one was ordered.

Shortly after Chief Bolger arrived he ordered a "Working fire'. Engine 43 and Ladder 20 were out of quarters and on the road in mere seconds since everyone was ready.

As we responded up Massachusetts Avenue and right on Columbia Road approaching the fire location I thought it odd that I couldn't see much of anything from my 'best seat in the house', the tiller seat.

When we turned left onto Hancock Street and rolled up to Rill St, the fire location, we saw that the fire had been in a 2 ½ story wood frame abandoned house. The house had been the location of several fires and actually now was just a large rubbish pile.

Chief Bolger explained to Lieutenant Paul McNiff that these first alarm companies had two fires previous to this one and he was sending them home. He instructed McNiff to oversee extinguishment and overhaul and that he would be back in about a half hour to dismiss us.

The Chief worried about his men and knew that he might need these companies to be refreshed for whatever else the next eight hours held in store for them. Our companies hadn't been busy yet tonight and he knew we wouldn't mind the extra work.

❧ ❧ ❧

Chief Bolger was turning sixty-five in February of 1982. He would have to retire on February 28th. One day tour he asked me to come up to the office. As I knocked on the screen door of District 7's office and entered, he proceeded to give me some news that I didn't really want to hear.

As part of the city's proposition 2½ bull shit the chiefs' aides were being done away with effective January 1st. He told me that since he was almost 65 he wasn't going to drive himself in two of the worst months of the winter. He would be retiring as of December 31st.

While that news meant that I was losing two months as his aide, I felt devastated that the best chief I had ever worked for was going to retire in less than one month.

For me, I was returning to Ladder 7 and was going to continue to respond to fires and actually work them, not just being the chief's aide. I was going to return to throwing ladders, opening roofs, ventilating, forcing entry and all of the other great work involved in being a truckie on the Boston Fire Department.

❧ ❧ ❧

Retired District Fire Chief Vincent A. Bolger passed away on January 31, 2011 at the age of 94.

Rest in Peace, Vinnie.

CHAPTER 50

Batman and Robin

After the retirement of Chief Vinnie Bolger, District 7, group 3 became the assignment of District Fire Chief James Freeman. Chief Freeman was another tremendously experienced and respected firefighter. He was a character unlike many others on the job.

Freeman had been a firefighter on Engine 12 in Roxbury for many years. After he was promoted to Fire Lieutenant he was assigned to Engine 24, also in Roxbury. Freeman's promotion to Fire Captain saw him assigned to Rescue 2, another Roxbury company and now he was a District Chief in District 7, one of the busiest districts in the city, located in Dorchester's Meeting House Hill.

Jim Freeman took as his aide Kenny Rogers who had once been an aide to District Chief Vinnie Bolger. Jimmy Freeman had briefly worked with Kenny when both were on Engine 24.

One of many things that they had in common was the following of the Boston Police on Kenny's scanner when they were working. They would wander about the district listening to police calls and sometimes getting the jump on an incident when the police may discover something when they were on routine patrol.

Since they had a habit of being seen at many police incidents the duo earned the nicknames 'Batman and Robin', the un-caped crime fighters. Even though they didn't actually take part in crime fighting, they were interested in potential fire department responses.

Chief Freeman also had two sons who became members of the Boston Police Department and a daughter-in-law who became a Fire Alarm Operator in Boston.

Did I mention that Kenny Rogers and Jimmy Freeman also worked a part-time job together servicing fire extinguishers? The dynamic duo spent a good deal of time together enjoying life to its fullest.

〜〜〜

Up until his days as a district chief's aide Kenny had spent all of his firefighting time on Engine 24, a banner fire company in Roxbury. Engine 24 was originally quartered by themselves at 434 Warren Street at the corner of Quincy Street in a firehouse constructed in 1873 and opened for service on December 10, of that year.

Engine 24 was just a dozen blocks down Warren Street from the Grove Hall neighborhood where Engine 13 and Ladder 23 were stationed.

On July 12, 1967 Engine 13 was assigned a second piece of apparatus, a rescue truck. The company became known as the Rescue Pumper Unit. (RPU) The RPU responded as both an engine company to first alarm responses and as a rescue company to rescue company responses in Division Two.

On October 25, 1972, the Rescue Pumper Unit was disbanded and the company became Rescue Company 2.

On August 16, 1973 Rescue 2 was moved down Blue Hill Avenue to the quarters of Engine 52 and Ladder 29 which was newly built and opened on June 27, 1973.

At this time, Engine 24's single firehouse at 434 Warren Street was closed for good and Engine 24 was relocated to 36 Washington Street with Ladder 23.

Today, both companies still operate out of this very busy firehouse in Grove Hall which was built in 1898 and opened for service on November 8 of that year as the quarters of Ladder 23 and the Deputy Chief of Division Three.

After March 31, 1954 there was no longer a Chief quartered in this firehouse and Ladder 23 was quartered alone until June 11, 1960 when Engine 13 came to stay for good. I must mention that there was a Lighting Plant quartered here intermittently.

Freeman and Rogers were paired at many incidents from 1982 until Freeman's retirement. I had the pleasure of working with them at Ladder 7 until my promotion and subsequent transfer in 1987.

Firefighter (Aide to Chief) Kenneth J. Rogers
retired on August 29, 2006.

Kenny, enjoy your retirement, you have earned it!

Retired District Fire Chief James J. Freeman
passed away on March 4, 2006.

Rest in Peace, Chief.

CHAPTER 51

St. Ambrose Church

One evening in January of 1984 the crew of Engine 17 and Ladder 7 had responded to an arson attempt at a dentist's office in Fields Corner on Dorchester Avenue. Someone had poured gasoline down the chimney from the rooftop of a one story block of stores, commonly referred to as a 'taxpayer'.

Taxpayer is an expression which was given to buildings which were erected on land owned by a property owner where the intent was to generate some income to pay the taxes on the land.

Most taxpayers are narrow depth, multi units in width and usually only one story in height. You will find many which have stores on the first floor and either offices or residential units on the second floor. Like most neighborhood shopping areas, Fields Corner was dotted with different taxpayers.

Fires in a block of stores were usually demanding. First off, in recent times, the storeowners were faced with increasingly high insurance premiums or perhaps they were unable to obtain insurance at all. Owners took all sorts of precautions to prevent theft, vandalism and arson. Some of the protection was in the form of roll-down shutters or grates, display windows and doors which had been reduced down to minimal openings and grated or solid coverings which were protected by case hardened steel padlocks. Glass replacement insurance premiums were obscenely high if you could get it at all.

One of the problems of all of this protection was a delay in detection of a fire in one of these stores. When finally detected the fire continued to grow as firefighters arrived at night and had to begin the forcible entry process.

Sometimes burglars and arsonists entered from the rear, but they were also known to make entry from the top down. In New York City it was not uncommon for store owners of high value properties and businesses to place sheets of steel on their roofs so that these criminal forces would not be able to cut through the roof and enter the businesses from above. We have not seen much of this in Boston.

When fires were initiated in the cellars of these buildings the firefight took on a much more complex tone. Ventilation of these areas was more difficult since entry had to be made from above. Firefighters were essentially entering down a chimney created by the natural process of the products of combustion. Cellar areas rarely had windows and exterior doors were few.

The search and rescue process had to be attempted since some of these store owners took to sleeping in their stores thereby combining business with residence. Some even rented out lodging as another source of income.

❧❧❧❧

On this particularly warm January evening we were mostly all inside of the dentist office when Tom McGovern came bursting in through the front door shouting that the church was on fire. You could just barely see the church across the street and down the next block. Everyone jumped on their respective companies and we proceeded down Dorchester Avenue, left on Lincoln St, left on Adams and up to the front of the church.

We had just recently drilled on the use of ladder pipes and in my head I thought that I would jump the sidewalk and attempt to throw the aerial over the cab and prepare for ladder pipe usage. Engine 17 stopped at a hydrant and between that and the potential collapse zone, I decided to take a position on the 'D' side of the church on Dickens Street.

As most church fires go, detection was delayed, large open areas created a much too hot and too far advanced fire condition. Sprinklers were unheard of when these old city churches were constructed at the turn of the previous century. Unfortunately this church was long gone when we arrived even though we were basically sitting across the street.

It broke my heart to watch the stained glass windows be broken into small shards of colored glass as the fire destroyed the church.

In September of 1980 St. William's Church burned. This church was just about a mile north of St. Ambrose Church, on Dorchester Avenue. One mile, two churches, two houses of worship destroyed.

CHAPTER 52

Tragic Senseless Deaths in the Line of Duty

The following are some of the traumatic Line of Duty deaths not covered in other chapters which occurred in the time frame covered by these stories.

Fire Lieutenant George J. Gottwald, Rescue Pumper Unit
Box 3-2124

Fire Lieutenant Gottwald died on March 3, 1970 after he collapsed upon exiting the fire building at 2235 Washington Street, Roxbury during an extremely stubborn cellar fire. He was a highly decorated member.

Fire Lieutenant Joseph J. Downing, Engine Company 2
Box 7316

Fire Lieutenant Joseph Downing died on October 16, 1970 from burns suffered on September 19, 1970 after a taxicab's gasoline tank exploded on Dorchester Street, South Boston. He had been burned over 90 percent of his body. Joe Downing had been a longtime member of Engine 43 before his promotion.

Firefighter Edwin H. Foley, Engine Company 30
Box 285

Firefighter Edwin H. 'Dicer' Foley died on December 30, 1970 after he alighted from the apparatus to investigate an alarm from Box 285. He slipped on a snow bank and fell under the wheels of Engine 30. This alarm proved to be false.

Firefighter Jeremiah Collins, Engine Company 45
Box 2593

Firefighter Jeremiah Collins ironically died on July 4, 1971 when a building in the Mt. Calvary Cemetery partially collapsed with the granite lintel crushing him while operating at Box 2593.

Fire Fighter James F. Doneghy, Ladder Company 30
Box 2388

Firefighter James F. Doneghy died on November 5, 1971 after being thrown from the tiller seat of Ladder 30 while responding to Box 2388.

Firefighter John A. Hopkins, Engine Company 34
Box 51

Fire Fighter John A. Hopkins died while detailed to Ladder 14 on May 11, 1972 when he was crushed between Ladder 14's truck and the door frame of the firehouse while responding to Box 51.

Firefighter Vincent Dimino, Ladder Company 30
Box 2394

Firefighter Vincent Dimino died on June 19, 1972 from injuries received earlier when he was thrown from the tiller seat of Ladder 30 while responding to Box 2394. This tragic death occurred only two days after the Hotel Vendome fire which killed nine members.

Firefighter Arthur L. Ceurvels, Ladder Company 20
Box 7311

Firefighter Arthur L. Ceurvels died on February 2, 1973 from injuries he received when Ladder 20's truck jack-knifed on the Southampton Street Bridge during a severe ice storm while responding to Box 7311.

Firefighter Bernard G. Tully, Engine Company 30
Still Alarm

Firefighter Bernard G. Tully died of injuries received on January 22, 1974 when Engine 30 and a rubbish truck collided on Centre St. in Roslindale on an extremely icy roadway.

Firefighter Richard P. Sheridan, Ladder Company 16
Box 3-2241

Firefighter Richard P. Sheridan was killed on October 23, 1976 while detailed to Aerial Tower 2 when a wall collapsed at a vacant factory at 22 Simmons Street, Roxbury.

Firefighter Robert M. Greene, Ladder Company 23
Box 3323

Firefighter Robert M. Greene died on November 27, 1978 when he fell from a building on Alpha Road in Dorchester.

CHAPTER 53

My Return to Division One

This chapter and the following one both tell short tales which occur after my first promotion, but I feel as though they have to be added here.

I have been promoted. It still seems like a dream. It took me 17 years, but here I am as a Fire Lieutenant. I am standing in Memorial Hall in Fire Headquarters with Bob Dorsey and Fred Sullivan being promoted to District Chief; Ed Lorenz and John Carey being promoted to Fire Captain; and Manny Arruda, Bobby Rull, Frank Jones and I being promoted to Fire Lieutenant.

As of January 2014 the only one of us still working is Frank Jones. Frank was promoted to lieutenant with me on March 4, 1987 and has since been promoted to captain and then district chief.

Frank is a great firefighter, outspoken, but experienced and extremely knowledgeable. I enjoyed working with him. One of my chauffeurs from my days on Rescue 1, John Cetrino, is now his aide.

John and Frank are a great pair. They worked together at Engine 33 in the Back Bay. There is no slowing John down whether it is working a fire or talking a fire.

I enjoyed my two regular chauffeurs while on Rescue One. First there was John Forristall and then John Cetrino. Most officers have the different members of a group rotate as drivers. My preference was to have a regular driver. My reasons were for their knowledge of the city, careful and observant driving skills and their comfort behind the wheel.

Today John Forristall is a captain assigned to the Special Operations Command, the unit which is responsible for all Technical Rescue disciplines. John is a perfect fit for this position with all of the classes and seminars that he has attended. I know that John would love to be in the field as a captain on a line company, but his skills are needed in the Special Ops Command right now. In time, as he is able to train other good instructors, he will be back in the field.

❧❧❧

While Ladder 20 was in Division One much of our running was to Division Two since the opposite side of the street from the firehouse was Division Two.

Ladder 7 was in Division Two. Now as a Fire Lieutenant I am heading back to Division One. While the stories stop here for now, I hope you will join me later when I recall my years as a company officer. I have plenty more stories. I just hope that there is an audience for me to tell them to.

God bless every one of you and please God, keep the brother firefighters safe.

CHAPTER **54**

The Liars Club

Even though this chapter jumps to my retirement years I feel as though it deserves a place in this book. Some of the greatest firefighters in the world still gather weekly to enjoy the friendships they made over the many years in which they dedicated their lives to the citizens of the City of Boston. Here is recognition to some of them, past and present.

).).).

Since I have retired I now am a member of an austere group known as the Liars Club. The club consists of retired members of the Boston Fire Department. Not all retired members attend Liars Club meetings, but all members are retired from the job.

As long as I can remember the Liars Club has met at the Training Academy on Moon Island. They meet Wednesday mornings for coffee and doughnuts. The entertainment is their tales from the past.

These fires that are rehashed by these characters become bigger and better every time they are told, hence 'The Liars Club'.

As I sit at the 'younger guys table' some Wednesday mornings I look about the room and realize what great company I have the honor of being with. The hundreds of years of experience of some of the most humble men in the world.

The number of lives saved by these men and their comrades over the years is staggering and probably unknown to anyone, but these guys are what the Boston Fire Department is all about.

We have special meetings with dinners at Christmas and on St. Patrick's Day. In September we take a trip to pay our respects to the nine firefighters who lost their lives at the Hotel Vendome fire on June 17, 1972. The monument is at the corner of Commonwealth Avenue and Dartmouth Street in the Back Bay section of Boston. The most beautiful monument dedicated to these nine men sits in the shadow of the Hotel Vendome.

❧❧❧

I remember one meeting where Jim Cosgrove mentioned that his wife, Sue, asked one Wednesday afternoon what the topic of the day had been.

Jimmy answered her query with, "This week it was surgeries. Last week it was prescriptions and the week before it was medical coverage."

❧❧❧

I could probably fill three pages with names of members from the past who attend meetings, but I'll only name a few from the present group.

Ex-Captain Leo 'Spanky' Sullivan is the official unelected superintendent in charge. 'Fabulous' Frank Feeney is the official coffee pourer and collector of the dues. Tommy Goodwin is Frank and Leo's assistant in charge of everything.

On any given Wednesday morning you may find Leo D. Stapleton, Sr. and Donald 'Tuck' Toomey holding court over the South End stories along with Ed Kavanaugh and John 'Bull' Heaney

Frank Barresi, Tom Clancy, Bill 'Pinky' Doyle, Eddie Fortey, Tony Serra, and Frank Spacco all gather around the 'hearing impaired guys' table where the voices bellow out so that each can be heard. Sirens and air horns over the years have taken a toll on all of our hearing.

Bill Noonan, Bill Twigg, Tom Matthews, Paul Canavan, Frank Greenberg, Herb Pearlstein, Paul Finn, Charlie Warnock, Mike King, and Steve McLaughlin all stop by weekly.

Jim Famolare, Ron Keating, Ed Loder, Larry Pelosi, Ron Richard, Fred Sullivan, Brian Touhy, and I like to join the others along with John Burden, Jim Cosgrove, and John Herr.

Gentlemen, I wish you all a happy, healthy and well-deserved retirement.

To Paul O'Brien, Maury LaCascia, and Steve 'Gus" Langone who have recently left us for the Liars Club in the sky; Rest in Peace Brothers.

They join Renzo Santangelo, Mickey Bowen, Arthur 'Schultzie' Howard, Harry Arnao, John Varner, Vinnie Gifford, and a host of others.

Brothers, May you all Rest in Peace.

About the Author

Richard 'Rick' Connelly is recently retired as a Fire Captain after 42 years of service to the Boston Fire Department.

Rick was a firefighter for seventeen years in the Brighton, South Boston, Roxbury and Dorchester neighborhoods of Boston before being promoted to lieutenant and then to captain where he worked in downtown Boston for twenty-five years.

He is the author of "Returning to Quarters". This is a history of every building ever used as a firehouse in the City of Boston and a history of all the companies that ever occupied them.

Rick lives in Stow, Massachusetts where he has enjoyed a few years being involved with the Stow, MA Fire Department as a call firefighter and captain.

He also spent nineteen years as an instructor at the Massachusetts Firefighting Academy in Stow.

Rick has five children with Hannah being the youngest and still at home. Rick Jr, Stacey, Amy and Pamela are all parents to their own families living in towns south of Boston.

His son, Rick Jr. of whom he is extremely proud is a firefighter/paramedic with the Hingham, MA Fire Department nearing ten years of service.

He is a grandfather to ten and a great grandfather to one. He is very proud of all of his children and their children.

CPSIA information can be obtained
at www.ICGtesting.com
Printed in the USA
FSOW03n2144081016
25900FS